PRAISE FOR T... ...IPLE

I love this nuanced and prac... ...runing *Principle* transforms the w... ...raction becomes a catalyst for deeper focus, clarity and actionable impact. Read this short powerhouse of a book and lean into effective change.

*Michael Fullan, OC, Professor Emeritus,
OISE/University of Toronto*

This highly practical book is an important antidote to the add-on mentality that overloads and burns out teachers and leaders.

*Distinguished Professor Emeritus Viviane Robinson,
University of Auckland*

At a time of increasing challenge in schools, this book gives down-to-earth, practical advice to help leaders reduce stress, manage workload and focus on the things that make the most difference. I loved it, and so will school leaders.

*Steve Munby, Visiting Professor,
University College London*

In a professional landscape where every priority feels equally crucial, this book offers simple and effective frameworks for generating positive momentum and helps schools focus on the right work in sustainable ways.

*Nicole West, Principal,
Inglewood Primary School, Western Australia*

Now a guide to the 'Art of Strategic Subtraction' – a powerful field guide to action.

Anthony Mackay, CEO,
Centre for Strategic Education Melbourne

Schools are the most important learning organisations in our communities, and improving their effectiveness, culture, and educational outcomes has a significant impact on students' lives. *The Pruning Principle* explores how educators can achieve sustainable improvement by mastering strategic subtraction, focusing on doing less but better to create a calmer, more effective school environment and, ultimately, improving student outcomes for all.

Shauna-Maree Sykes, General Manager,
Education, Strategy and Performance,
Melbourne Archdiocese Catholic Schools

Simon and Michael have highlighted a solution to one of education's biggest problems – educators are overloaded! The idea of mastering strategic subtraction, rather than the "endless wheel of doing more", makes this book a must-read for any leader seeking to break free from overload and refocus on maximising impact within their school.

Dr Ryan Dunn, Senior Lecturer,
Faculty of Education, Melbourne University

In our school world of increased complexity and workload, *The Pruning Principle* is both a refreshing perspective on how to work better and a step-by-step guide to achieving what we all want the most – better outcomes for our students, our staff and ourselves.

Courtney Howard, Principal,
Cambridge Primary School, Tasmania

The Pruning Principle

MASTERING THE ART OF
STRATEGIC SUBTRACTION
WITHIN EDUCATION

The Pruning Principle

**DR SIMON BREAKSPEAR
AND MICHAEL ROSENBROCK**

amba press

Published in 2024 by Amba Press, Melbourne, Australia
www.ambapress.com.au

© Dr Simon Breakspear and Michael Rosenbrock

All rights reserved. No part of this book may be reproduced or transmitted in any form or by any means, electronic or mechanical, including photocopying, recording or by any information storage and retrieval system, without prior permission in writing from the publisher.

Cover design: Tess McCabe
Internal design: Amba Press
Developmental editor: Jaimee Vilela
Editor: Andrew Campbell

ISBN: 9781923215405 (pbk)
ISBN: 9781923215412 (ebk)

A catalogue record for this book is available from the National Library of Australia.

CONTENTS

Preface: Why We Wrote This Book — vii
Acknowledgements — viii
About the Authors — ix
Introduction: Doing Fewer Things Better — 1

Part 1: The Pruning Principle — 5

Chapter 1	The Additive Trap	7
Chapter 2	The Pruning Principle	17
Chapter 3	The Pruning Cycle	31
Chapter 4	Pruning Mindset Shifts	51
Chapter 5	Running Pruning Experiments	59

Part 2: Pruning in Action — 69

Chapter 6	Personal Pruning	71
Chapter 7	Pruning Meetings	85
Chapter 8	Pruning Professional Development	101
Chapter 9	Pruning Improvement Plans	117
Chapter 10	Subtractive Solution Sessions	127

Conclusion — 135
Appendices — 141
References — 147
Index — 151

PREFACE
WHY WE WROTE THIS BOOK

Someone asked me recently, "After working with 100,000 educational leaders, if you could download one thing into the minds of all of them, *The Matrix*-style, what would it be?" My answer? "Learn to say no to things, in order to do fewer things well." It's not an overstatement to say that I genuinely believe the Pruning Principle explained in this book has the power to unlock the next phase of improvement in our schools and bring a new era of sustainability to our workforce.

In this book you'll find a set of ideas and practical tools that will help you apply the Pruning Principle in your own teams, and reap the rewards of better focus, sustained energy, and a sense of meaningful progress. I can't wait to hear how you adapt and apply these ideas in your own unique educational context.

Towards better learning,

Simon Breakspear
June 2024

ACKNOWLEDGEMENTS

We are immensely grateful to the leaders and teachers who generously partner with us to understand persistent challenges and surface new insights. *The Pruning Principle* emerged from embedded work seeking practical solutions to our schools' challenges of overload and overwhelm.

Sincere thanks to Jaimee Vilela for your patience in refining and editing the full manuscript. You've brought clarity to our writing and injected joy throughout the process. This book would have been stuck in our heads and slide decks without you.

To Alicia and the Amba Press team, thank you for your belief in the project and your speed and skill in helping us get these ideas and tools into the hands of educators.

We are grateful to our families for putting up with us during the intense writing process and inspiring us to do what we do, which is to enable sustainable education system change.

Simon Breakspear and Michael Rosenbrock

ABOUT THE AUTHORS

Dr Simon Breakspear is a researcher, advisor and speaker on educational leadership, policy and change. Simon develops frameworks and tools that make evidence-based ideas actionable and easy to understand. Over the last decade, his capability-building work has given him the opportunity to work with over 100,000 educators across more than ten countries.

Simon is an Adjunct Senior Lecturer in the School of Education at UNSW. He has served as an advisor to the NSW Department of Education and sits on an expert steering committee for the Australian Institute for Teaching and School Leadership (AITSL). Simon received his BPsych (Hons) from UNSW, his MSc in Comparative and International Education from the University of Oxford, and his PhD in Education from the University of Cambridge. He has been a Commonwealth and Gates Scholar. Simon began his work in education as a high school teacher.

Michael Rosenbrock is an experienced and passionate educational leader, accomplished facilitator and advisor, and a teacher of physics, science, mathematics and multimedia. He partners with people and organisations with a focus on work that has potential to improve the lives and opportunities of children and young people.

Michael regularly works with systems, networks, school leaders and teachers across sectors and jurisdictions in Australia. He is a passionate advocate for those experiencing socio-economic disadvantage and for students in rural, regional and remote settings. Prior to working in schools, Michael worked in the aerospace, automotive and software industries in Germany, the USA and Australia. Michael holds a Bachelor of Aerospace Engineering and a Bachelor of Business from RMIT University, and a Graduate Diploma of Education from Monash University.

Contributors

We are very grateful to the educators listed here who have contributed to the development of the Pruning Principle framework, tested tools, and provided some practitioner insights and tips throughout the text.

- Angela Dawson
- Hayley Dureau
- Dr Charlotte Forwood
- Martha Goodridge-Kelly
- Leia Hands
- Michelle Heintze-Moller
- Chanel Herring
- Veronica Hoy
- Nicole Jasinowicz
- Sarah Kubik
- Christine Lambrianidis
- Justine Mackey
- Daniel McMahon
- David Muzyk
- Nicole West

More information about the Pruning Principle and links to online resources throughout the book can be found at **https://pruningprinciple.com**

INTRODUCTION
DOING FEWER THINGS BETTER

Schools are the most consequential organisations in our modern society. The stakes couldn't be higher for us in seeing them thrive. As educators, we know that improving our schools' effectiveness, culture and educational outcomes by even a fraction each year could have a significant, rippling impact on the learning and life outcomes of our students. The reality, though, is that we have finite time, money, energy and human resources to play with in order to get there, and every day requires us to make new trade-offs with competing priorities.

Many leaders express a desire to feel calm, in control, and on top of things. We speak often about wanting to support educator wellbeing, and lead a "calmer school", with fantastic rhythms and an achievable workload. However, the problem for most of us is that we don't have shared language, processes, tools or rhythms for how to actually get there.

As we know, we cannot summon more financial and human resources for ourselves by magic; we can only spend what we have as wisely as we can. But therein lies the problem: the way we are working isn't working. We all know it, and we often speak about it. But we can't seem to find our way off the relentless wheel of "doing more". We've stretched our time, energy and resources so thinly that many schools are being crushed by the weight of everything they're trying to achieve. It's simply no longer sustainable.

What if the answer to this conundrum and to unlocking our next stage of improvement in education was to be found in an unlikely place – horticulture? We believe that the Pruning Principle, otherwise known as the art of mastering strategic subtraction, holds the vital key for educators to be able to set and maintain achievable work rhythms and unlock real gains in school improvement. The Pruning Principle is, first and foremost, about seeking the best for our learners through the disciplined pursuit of doing less – but better[1].

How to use this book

Our hope is that you use this book like a field guide to action. We feel confident that the ideas, framework and tools included are robust and user-friendly, ready for practical application in your own context.

The book has two key parts:

In Part 1, we explore the why, what and how of pruning. In Chapter 1, we outline the concept of "the additive trap" and the factors that have landed us here. In Chapter 2, we unpack the Pruning Principle and the underlying mechanisms that make pruning effective. In Chapter 3, we provide a detailed overview of the three stages of the Pruning Cycle and unpack the specific steps teams can take to implement it. In Chapter 4, we unpack the enabling mindset shifts we will need to put pruning into action. Chapter 5 explores running pruning experiments to reduce stress and increase safety as we begin.

Part 2 of the book – Pruning in Action – details what pruning can look like in the real world. Each chapter unpacks a specific use case of pruning, including the steps and tools that make it easier to do. You can see Part 2 as your "pruning starter pack", which will illustrate potential ways to implement your new pruning practice. Treat each chapter as some inspiration for your pruning experiments.

---

1 The concepts of pruning and strategic subtraction have a connection to the field of de-implementation. See Appendix A.

In Chapter 6, we explore personal workload pruning. In Chapter 7, we explain how to begin pruning meetings. In Chapter 8, we delve into pruning our professional learning. In Chapter 9, we discuss pruning improvement plans. In Chapter 10, we approach subtractive solutions to complex problems.

For each, we've suggested some tools and processes that might support your work through the three phases of the pruning cycle. However, you should remember that pruning is not a lock-step defined process – you're welcome to adapt and innovate it for yourself as you need to. You need to trust your instincts about how you might best achieve these goals within your unique context. If you like a tool, use it! If you want to adapt a tool, go for it! If you would prefer to head your own way and build a different collective protocol, please share your thinking back with us!

We hope you can use this book as a playbook to set you and your team on your own path towards greater focus, simplicity and calmness. Feel free to dip in and out of different sections over time as you develop your mastery of pruning and are looking to enhance your skills or respond to specific challenges that emerge.

PART 1

The Pruning Principle

CHAPTER 1
THE ADDITIVE TRAP

A STATE OF FRENZIED STAGNATION

Are you busier than you were three years ago? For how many years would you say this has been true? When we examine the sheer number of programs, projects and commitments we find ourselves tied to in our schools, it's easy to see why the overload is real. We have found ourselves in a state of "frenzied stagnation", where doing more is the default, yet it's not having the impact we hope that it will. Stagnation is defined as a prolonged period of little or no progress, and it's ironic that we've found ourselves here given the maddening pace most of us face in our roles. When we walk into a school and ask the educators we're working with how everyone is going, someone will invariably reply with something like, "Oh, crazy busy." We'll say, "Extra crazy busy, or normal crazy busy?" They'll say "Just normal, crazy busy." The reality is that being overloaded, exhausted and depleted is the new normal, and we've rewired our brains to accept this and believe that is how it has to be. As one educational leader in my local school system said to me recently, "I've been flat out all week. I'm exhausted, and I don't think I've even achieved anything." We know he's not alone.

We fail to understand the true impact of overload on our organisation and the overall quality of our working lives. Schools, teams and system teams have become like a laptop that's been on for weeks or even a couple of months without being switched off – running slow, with too many applications going in the background, and 34 tabs open from articles we promised ourselves we'd get to "at some point". Still, we don't feel like we can risk turning it off – to begin again feels risky, in case we lose something important. It feels like we are always out of time, and before we are out of time, we are out of cognitive and emotional energy. We find ourselves jumping from one thing to another and never feeling we are making meaningful progress, all while running at a steady state of using 120% of our available capacity. So, how did we get ourselves into this state?

We're dealing with "the additive trap".

1.1 The additive trap

Why we are busier than ever

The additive trap in education refers to a tendency to engage in improvement by defaulting to adding one more thing. We are like a calculator with only one function: addition. Our individual and team rhythms, tools, templates, protocols and conversational norms are focused on how best to improve our schools through additive actions. The default assumption is that pursuing improvement for our students, staff and systems implicitly means doing *more things*.

We all know what it feels like to fall into the trap of spending all of our time in meetings, or coordinating, emailing, checking in, following up, completing a template, having a 1:1 conversation – whatever it may be – *about* the work, but not feeling like we can progress the things that we need to do. It's as if we have declared inbox and calendar bankruptcy, and proceed to just add more anyway. We are in an additive trap in education. It's not sustainable, and it's self-defeating. Schools are long-term institutions, which means there's no point in having "a good term" or quarter; effective leadership is about focusing on how best to set up our schools to really thrive for the long term – and for us and our teams to thrive in our roles while we're at it.

So why do we, as educators, tend to fall for the additive trap and land ourselves in a state of frenzied stagnation?

Educator workload

So much to do and so little time. Similar sentiments are commonplace in education across settings and borders. This is not new, and the issue has endured for many years. Average working hours for both leaders and teachers are commonly described as unmanageable, unachievable, unsustainable (Heffernan et al., 2019; Horowitz et al., 2024; NSW Department of Education, 2017) and significantly exceeding contracted hours (Australian Institute for Teaching and School Leadership, 2024). High workload, poor work-life balance, and associated stress are consistently identified as issues by the profession (Horowitz et al., 2024; OECD, 2021) and are frequently the reasons given for educators leaving the profession prior to retirement (Australian Institute for Teaching and School Leadership, 2024; Education Endowment Foundation, 2023; Heffernan et al., 2019; OECD, 2021). This is more than a workforce satisfaction issue – with workload impacting negatively on the capacity of both leaders and teachers to do their core work of improving outcomes for students (Hunter et al., 2021; OECD, 2021).

We can't have it all: We are playing a never-ending game of trade-offs

Every day, we need to make trade-offs. The concept of trade-offs, as we know, is a fundamental principle in economics, decision-making, and everyday life. It's about making decisions that require us to balance competing outcomes, benefits or costs. Having a deep understanding of the trade-offs we are making is essential for effective decision-making and allocating our resources wisely. For those of us in education, making trade-offs means acknowledging that any additional activities or commitments that we add on have to come out of somewhere else – existing time, resources and energy that would have otherwise gone towards other things. This is crucial, and it's something that we tend to forget. With each new thing we add, over time we're asking ourselves to do more things with the same amount of resources. This is the nature of the beast, and it's a way of working that is simply not sustainable, nor effective.

1.2 Let's just add one more thing

We have paired caring with "doing more"

Firstly, we got to this point *because we care*.

In our vocation as educators, we care deeply about our students, about our schools, and about the uniquely powerful place we know our schools hold in shaping the next generation. The stakes of getting education right couldn't be higher for our students and broader society. We don't take this lightly. So we contend with a gnawing sense of false guilt over needing to do *more* for our students and more for our schools. We've bought into a misguided belief that "more is always better", even when this results in highly fragmented energy and focus. We tell ourselves that to pull back on activity is akin to giving up – that it proves we can't, or are unwilling, to "do what it takes". The irony of this is that the very attitude that has led us to do so well in improving our schools thus far – caring deeply – has gotten us to the point where we are constantly adding new things at the expense of our productivity and effectiveness.

Humans have a natural tendency to think that improvement equals addition

The second point is that doing more is in our very nature. When we try to solve problems or lift outcomes, humans generally tend to overlook subtractive answers and instead focus on how to improve something by adding more to it (Adams et al., 2021). A good example of this is our typical travel itinerary. Have you ever been planning an extended overseas holiday and, with the goal of making the most of the trip, found yourself adding on an extra city, country or stop? By the end, you realise you've created an overloaded, exhausting travel itinerary, with the only result of the trip being that you now know where you want to revisit the next time you go back. What about hosting a dinner party? You want to impress, you want to make sure there's variety, and you have to cover every dietary requirement. What do you do? Add fries with that, then side salads, and a buttery mash! Before you know it, your table is so laden with extra food you find yourself eating leftovers for lunch in the common room for a week. Adding is in our nature, and as we keep proving to ourselves, we don't know when to stop.

Through a range of experimental approaches, psychologists have studied the fact that humans systematically overlook subtractive changes. In one synthesis article published in *Nature*, the authors explain that when asked to improve something, whether it's a Lego structure, a golf course, an essay, or solving a puzzle, humans tend to suggest adding new things, rather than stripping back what's already there – even when those additions lead to objectively subpar results. Interestingly, when people are distracted and overloaded, they're even more likely to produce an additive rather than a subtractive answer (Adams et al., 2021).

We landed ourselves in the additive trap through a simple assumption: that if we are to solve problems and improve the things that matter most in schools, we should continue everything we are currently doing and then add one more thing. We have rhythms and routines, templates and approaches to school improvement to ensure that every term, year or three-to-four-year planning cycle, we carry out all the things we've already committed to, while adding additional projects or initiatives that theoretically will finally give us the breakthrough that we need.

> **We landed ourselves in the additive trap through a simple assumption: that if we are to solve problems and improve the things that matter most in schools, we should continue everything we are currently doing and then add one more thing.**

There are more things than ever

Those of us working in education throughout 2020–23 will also have experienced the very real post-pandemic overload. The additive trap became worse, not better, after our once-in-100-years shock to the system. The pandemic was a pause. We heard the birds again. We played board games and card games, and we were home midweek for family meals. But the particular challenge for those of us in education over those years is that with the disruption of the pandemic, many of us experienced a significant pause in the number of things we were doing. However, most of us didn't take the opportunity – or feel we had the freedom or tools – to do any pruning. This meant that on the other side of the crisis, we experienced a dramatic return to all the things we used to do in our schools, *plus* a range of additional new work in wellbeing, behaviour and learning that we then committed to do in the aftermath. The one lesson we were meant to learn from the pandemic was the danger of running a system at full or above full capacity – you always need to leave a margin for the unexpected. Yet we found ourselves even more overloaded than we had been before.

1.3 Each thing we add is bigger than we anticipate it will be

We underestimate the hidden costs of each new thing

On top of maintaining the good things that we've already embedded each year, we're busy adding new things. The problem is that, when doing this, we often overlook the hidden cost of the coordination and effort each additional thing we take on will require of us. We might consider whether or not the budget can absorb the costs, but we tend not to systematically work through the human demands of additional programs and initiatives. We underestimate the extra overhead costs of time and energy these new commitments will necessitate, taxing us of our time and energy – like the email surcharge, the coordination levy, and the thinking and cognitive switching costs. We are often caught off guard later when each new program, task or priority rears its head and requires more from us. We fail to pause and pay attention to the very real challenges of what it will actually look like in our workflow.

All of this, of course, has been made more challenging by the digitisation of education, which means that the demands of everything we commit to can now seep into all corners of our work week. We are more connected in schools than ever, with the option for classes online, forums, and a seemingly endless number of channels to communicate through. Aside from the obvious upsides to this comes the felt expectation by teachers and school leaders to be "always on". It's now much harder to switch off, when there's always a text, Teams message, or email to reply to.

> **Initiative overload**
>
> A common theme in discussions with educators is "initiative overload". This extends beyond change fatigue or resistance to change. It is about being asked to put in place too many new things, too quickly. Both school leaders and teachers identify "frequent initiatives" as one of the top barriers to the core work of teaching (Hunter et al., 2021) – and this is far from a new issue (Curtis, 2003). Sometimes this comes down to system initiatives and policies, which flow through to schools. To an extent school leaders can be judicious in their buffering and shielding to reduce the impact this has on teachers – finding ways to fit the new into the existing, and prioritising what is needed now against what can happen later. However, other parts of this overload come from formal and informal ways that we as leaders are primed to add new things. These can arise with each yearly improvement cycle, school review or new strategic plan – or after attending a compelling leadership conference session, reading an inspiring book, or having a bit too much thinking time while mowing the lawn. Regardless of our role and level of influence, the pervasive nature of the issue of "initiative overload" should give us pause for thought before we commit to adding anything else to what we do, or what we ask others to do.

We overlook the long-term maintenance effort

Lastly, we tend to overlook the fact that maintaining our existing suite of commitments, without dropping any of the balls in the air, takes serious work in itself. We need to be cognisant of what it takes not just to do the new thing, but to do it while continuing to do the things we've already been doing, well. Take the example of buying a new car. There's nothing more exciting than picking up a fresh set of keys and inhaling that new car smell. But who among us has not found it immensely frustrating every year to make sure we book it for a service? Between finding the time to do it, dropping it off and picking it up at an inconvenient time of day – not to mention the monetary cost – maintenance can be high maintenance! The same is true for putting in a new lawn. The initial tasks of preparing the soil, laying the grass, and daily watering for the first few weeks may seem like where the bulk of the effort lies. But of course, it is actually the long-term care – watering, cutting and fertilising through changing seasons over many years – where the vast majority of the effort is to be found.

It's the same in our schools. We tend to overlook the long-term maintenance levels required to keep the things we've already committed to running and sustaining impact. This means we wind up spending more time in meetings and in our inbox than actually doing the work.

1.4 Trying to do more with less

We are operating in a resource-constrained environment

While we have been beavering away adding more things to our workload, the resources available to carry out our priorities, programs and practices are becoming more limited.

There are more limited financial resources available to us now – post-pandemic constraints in public and private spending on education have meant that many schools are trying to do more with less. In many countries, school budgets have been shrunk, placing extra pressure on the collaborative time, professional learning, and external expertise we have typically relied on to do our jobs well.

We also know that in our industry there are more challenges with human resources now than ever. There are the realities of teacher shortages, and challenges with finding sufficient substitute teachers. There is also another interesting factor at play: the changing social contract between the newer generation of educators and the system. Educators are waking up to the fact that giving endless hours leads only to burnout and decreased efficiency, and have begun to push back on doing so. In Australia, certain states and school systems are now imposing set hours for teachers, after which paid overtime is applicable. Other teachers are starting to put up stronger personal boundaries around what they will and will not do beyond the core activities of the job. All of this means there is less discretionary time and energy available to go towards the ever-growing list of things we are committing ourselves to.

Even to sustain what we are currently doing, without adding anything further, will be impossible in the context of diminishing financial and human resource availability.

1.5 Beyond the additive trap

So the question is, how can we learn to *stop doing things*? How might we collectively interrupt this cycle and avoid falling into the additive trap that we seem stuck in now in our schools? We cannot keep grinding ourselves down to nothing. It is an unsustainable and, indeed, ultimately counter-productive way of pursuing long-term meaningful change.

IN SUMMARY

- We are busier than ever in education because we have continued adding to our commitments and initiatives without creating space to reflect and subtract – leaving us in a state of frenzied stagnation that is impacting our health, wellbeing and effectiveness.

- This is because we've paired caring with adding – we care about solving problems and optimising our impact for

learners, so we've simply continued to add more things in the hope of improvement.
- As humans, we tend to default to trying to improve something by adding to it.
- We also overlook the hidden costs of each new thing we commit to, and the ongoing maintenance costs of what we're already doing.
- We are facing a landscape of contracting financial and human resources.

ON REFLECTION

- Where do you experience the additive trap occurring in your team, school or system? In which areas does it feel most tempting to continue to add new things?
- What are the major internal drivers of the additive trap in your context?
- What percentage of your improvement conversations and strategies are additive versus subtractive in nature currently?
- How many strategies in your current improvement plan are subtractive changes – things that you are deliberately working to reduce or remove?
- What proportion of your work is maintenance of what you are already doing?
- When you think of the "email surcharge", the "coordination levy", the "people management tax" – which ones do you regularly overlook when adding new commitments, initiatives and priorities?

CHAPTER 2
THE PRUNING PRINCIPLE

2.1 The potential of pruning within education

So, where might we look for a solution to this frenzy we find ourselves in? Normally, we would turn to the psychological literature to seek insights that could inform a workable solution in schools. However, this time, the most helpful approach came from a most unexpected field: horticulture. Prepare your secateurs, because it turns out that the same principles and practices of pruning that apply to dynamic ecosystems have broader relevance.

The ancient Greeks and Romans played pivotal roles in developing early pruning techniques (National Geographic Society, 2024). Their pioneering efforts in horticulture highlight their deep understanding of plant biology and a commitment to optimising growth and productivity.

In ancient Greece, pruning was an essential practice in olive groves, a cornerstone of their economy. They understood that regular pruning was crucial for the health and productivity of olive trees. By removing dead or diseased branches and shaping the tree for better sunlight exposure, they ensured robust growth and a good harvest. Greek farmers developed specific techniques and tools for different pruning tasks, emphasising precision and timing.

The Romans took the Greeks' agricultural knowledge and expanded upon it, particularly in their vineyards and orchards. One of the most notable figures in Roman agriculture was Pliny the Elder. In his extensive work *Natural History*, Pliny mentions the importance of pruning (Pliny, n.d.). He emphasises that the right timing and technique in pruning can significantly enhance the yield and quality of fruit. The Romans recognised that pruning was not just about removing unwanted growth, but about strategically guiding the plant's development. They used a variety of tools, each designed for specific cuts and types of plants. For instance, they had curved knives for precise cuts, and saws for thicker branches. Their methods were so refined that many principles still apply today.

Believe it or not, these concepts are incredibly useful for those of us in education who are trying to work through how to get beyond a state of overload and make long-term meaningful progress. At the core of the Pruning Principle is a flip in the fundamental logic of educational impact: that in doing less you can achieve more over the long term. The Pruning Principle is all about mastering the art of strategic subtraction. We define the Pruning Principle in the context of education: *Deliberately cutting off or cutting back is essential to cultivating long-term vitality and impact.*

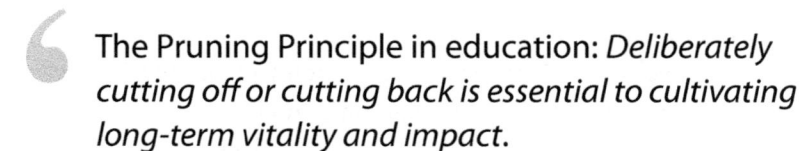

> **The Pruning Principle in education:** *Deliberately cutting off or cutting back is essential to cultivating long-term vitality and impact.*

What makes pruning interesting is that it involves an artful balancing act of both removal and preservation. If you're descended from a gardener or have a bit of a green thumb, you'll know that the core purpose of pruning a plant is redirecting energy and resources. Pruning also stimulates desired new growth, and reshapes the plant or tree for health and longevity. When applied to our context, the concept of pruning is about zooming out and taking stock of the raft of activities, commitments and projects – at individual, team, organisational and system levels – and finding opportunities to prune back on activities that are inefficient, ineffective or underperforming, to set ourselves up for new growth. The reality is that when we don't prune, the result is unbridled growth, which actually leads to less long-term positive growth. The absence of pruning equates to a decision to reduce long-term growth, though it's likely that many of us haven't thought about the consequences.

To learn to prune well, we must believe that we will flourish when we expose ourselves and our organisations to frequent pruning. This is counter-cultural in educational circles – indeed, for some, the idea is almost sacrilegious! We will need to approach this collectively. It has to be done together.

The Pruning Principle connects intentional subtraction with our long-term aspirations for our schools and thus helps us to break through the unhealthy and unsustainable additive trap. It's important, too, that we don't confuse pruning with doing nothing. While leaving something alone for a while, or putting a pause on adding anything else, can be useful in the short term, this is not as impactful or important as active, thoughtful pruning. Pruning is a deliberate act – it is not the same as just "not adding". It is a decision based on the belief that in living ecosystems like schools, intentional subtraction will result in more of the long-term outcomes we truly want. It involves thinking more in the short term about what matters, and it takes seriously the need to use fewer resources than you have, not more. We are convinced that pruning is vital to protecting and nourishing the long-term organisational health and impact of our schools.

Applying the Pruning Principle involves understanding the three key underlying mechanisms of pruning, plus embracing the need to embed regular rhythms of pruning at different levels of our roles and influence.

2.2 Pruning mechanisms: What pruning actually does

In the context of horticulture, the goal of pruning is to improve a garden over time through a process of cutting back. But to do this effectively with precision and care – and to understand how the concept of pruning could apply to us more broadly – we need to understand the underlying mechanisms that actually produce the benefits. How is it that pruning something back can yield more fruit and lead to a healthier tree? It's both counterintuitive and intriguing.

Here are the mechanisms of pruning in horticulture, and you'll soon notice how they translate directly in putting the Pruning Principle to work in schools. We're not talking about tools for pruning yet here, we are focusing on how pruning has its impact – the mechanisms themselves.

Figure 2.1: Pruning mechanisms

Redirects
finite energy
and resources

Stimulates
desired
new growth

Reshapes
for health
and longevity

First, pruning *redirects* finite energy and resources

In a plant or garden, there are finite resources available – just as there are in our schools. The act of pruning redirects the resources that a plant has available, freeing them up so that they can make their highest possible contribution to the overall health of the plant. It's about maximising what you can achieve with what you have; quality over quantity.

Removing dead, diseased or damaged growth is the first priority when it comes to pruning a plant. Cutting off unhealthy parts of a plant stops the issue from getting worse, but, crucially, it also diverts additional precious resources towards the plant's core goal: trying to stay alive. It gives the plant the best chance possible for healthy, productive growth.

A young plant is particularly vulnerable as it establishes itself. Pruning plants in this stage redirects their resources to establishing strong roots, structure and foliage so they are well placed to thrive into the future. This may mean removing growth and fruit, which can feel counterintuitive, but is essential for making sure the plant's resources go to the place where they can have the most benefit.

So how might this apply to the health of a school? In schools we are often establishing and nurturing things that are important and that have great potential for making an impact. Applying the Pruning Principle in our context – whether to a program, practice, team or person – means cutting back on what is not absolutely necessary, in order to focus resources on establishing a strong foundation. When done well, this can be a critical decision that ensures future longevity and impact. We'd start by evaluating any activities that are having a negative impact, not working, or not working as well as they could be. We'd then decide which ones need to go so that we can redirect those valuable resources to things that will better help us meet our goals.

Pruning activity doesn't equate to reducing resources

It's important to note that pruning is not about reducing the financial or human resources available to schools. Returning to the analogy of a garden, the act of pruning isn't about providing less water, sunlight or nutrients to a plant. Rather, it's about thinking about how to best redirect the existing energy and resources to the things most likely to lead to the desired impact. In educational settings, this means that we should begin pruning without fear that it will lead to our resources being reduced. The act of pruning requires that the same level of resourcing should be sustained so that we have capacity to nurture what has been pruned.

Second, pruning *stimulates* desired new growth

Put simply, pruning a plant is something we choose to do because it produces a better result than leaving the tree alone. This is confirmed by thousands of years of human knowledge in horticulture, which serves as a helpful guide to us on what and how to prune in order to get the best result. By carefully selecting the growth that we stimulate through pruning, we can increase both the quantity and quality of fruit produced. In our context in education, we can similarly apply our deep knowledge of educational practice plus our own context, and leverage the art of pruning to produce even better outcomes.

Counterintuitively, there are times when this may mean cutting back on something that is going well. To encourage fruit quality, we may remove branches, buds or young fruit so that the plant grows fewer but higher-quality fruit. This can feel incredibly uncomfortable at first – think about plucking off beautiful blossoms or baby fruit. But doing so produces better results. In a school, it's common for us to have many programs, priorities, opportunities and initiatives with potential, but not the infinite resources to do everything well at once. This means that sometimes we need to make an informed judgement about what has the greatest potential to produce a future benefit for our school – and cut back on some other things that are going well, so we can do fewer things better.

> **Practitioner insight!**
>
> As I'm putting the Pruning Principle into practice in my school I can see how similar it is to my strawberry patch at home. The plants produce heaps of flowers, but if I want a good harvest, I need to pick off the weaker flowers early on so that the plant puts its energy into the strongest and healthiest growth. My kids get upset about pulling off the beautiful flowers, but it is how we get a great harvest of strawberries.
>
> – *Daniel McMahon (Principal in Australia)*

Another interesting facet of pruning that we can learn from is that established plants sometimes need more substantial pruning to rejuvenate them and restore their vigour. This obviously needs to be done carefully and strategically, working within the limits of the plant and applying expert knowledge of how best to stimulate renewal. In a school we may have established programs, practices or processes that are stagnating – things that may have once produced a significant benefit but may now just be using up resources. For example, certain administrative processes may have become unwieldy and time-consuming, or a particular approach to collaboration or professional development may have reached a point of stagnation. You may still need these things, but their form may change. Looking closely at what is well established can help to identify where we can strategically cut back, to redirect energy into what makes an impact.

Third, pruning *reshapes* for health and longevity

Reshaping takes time and requires having a clear vision of the end result. It is driven by a deep understanding of purpose, and keeping our eyes on what is of the utmost long-term value.

Pruning is a long game. When we deliberately cultivate the shape of a plant over time, we're supporting it to live a long, healthy and productive life. For us in schools, this speaks to the strategic decisions we make to cut off or cut back, so that what we do is sustainable and produces the best possible future outcome. The current leaders of schools are the stewards of their institutions and have a responsibility to leave them in a position to flourish over the long term, rather than collapse under the weight of their own growth.

Deliberately reshaping a plant can help it to develop a form or structure that is more likely to be healthy and productive over time. We might choose to keep branches growing at a certain angle that are more likely to be strong and less likely to snap off the trunk in a heavy wind. Or we may thin out some areas to allow for better light and airflow. In a school, this means taking in the complete picture of all that is happening now, plus our visions for the future. With the end goal in mind, we can then start looking at which areas may need reshaping to ensure our long-term success.

This may also involve removing things that we can already see are going to become problematic – branches that will begin to rub on each other and create wounds that can eventually lead to disease. Pre-empting this requires us to stay vigilant – in the garden and in schools alike. Organisational norms around communication and resolving issues can be important for addressing this. Leaders cannot always spot problems in the earliest stage, so establishing a culture where staff feel empowered to bring these to light is crucial.

Reshaping can also be a practical measure. It might be because we want to maintain a size that doesn't impact on other plants and enables fruit to readily be harvested. In schools, like any organisation, processes and practices can become unwieldy and ineffective – like a jumbled tangle of branches. Sometimes we need to reconsider not just what we are doing, but also how. For example, do we still need those meetings? Are there activities we are guilty of continuing "because we've always done them", without reference to their current impact?

2.3 Pruning levels and pruning rhythms

Pruning can be applied at different levels

The Pruning Principle can be applied at all levels in education, from our personal workload all the way up to system level. It's less about the scale of what is pruned, or the effect, but rather the level that you are focusing your perspective and actions on. It's relevant at every level of our organisations.

- **Personal** pruning can be a great place to get started and involves a focus on our workflow, roles and responsibilities. It is the level where we often have the most agency and influence to make subtractive change.

- **Team**-level pruning focuses on the processes, priorities and ways of working of a specific team. It often involves a relatively small group that works together in a specific capacity and requires collective decision-making. This can be a fertile context for building a subtractive culture that is then able to be scaled to the rest of the organisation.

- **Organisational**-level pruning focuses on the organisation as a whole, looking at strategic priorities and how our efforts interconnect across the entire organisation. This is often led at a leadership level, but involves and impacts everyone.

- **System**-level pruning looks beyond the scope of a single organisation and can involve pruning at the policy, priority, program or initiative level. The scale of change at this level can vary in size; however, due to the broad scope the impact can be significant.

Figure 2.2: Levels of pruning

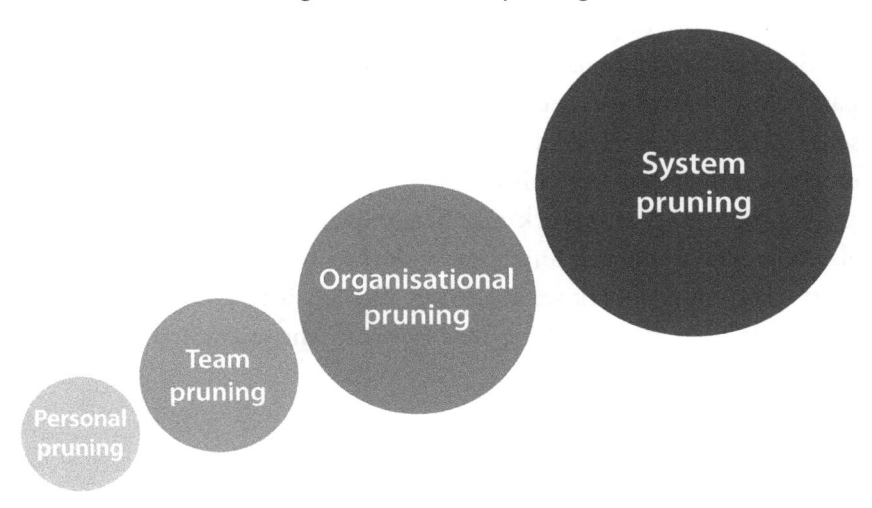

[Diagram showing five overlapping circles of increasing size labeled: Personal pruning, Team pruning, Organisational pruning, System pruning]

At each of these levels there are a wide range of areas that might be productive targets for pruning, including: priorities, commitments, strategies, projects, programs, initiatives, activities, processes and practices.

Setting up pruning rhythms

Pruning isn't a one-off activity. The three-step cycle we will outline in Chapter 3 should be repeated regularly at the different levels of personal workflow, teams, organisations, networks and systems. We should seek to establish regular pruning rhythms for ourselves that become baked into our workflow, so that we're not trying to do a one-off deep prune every few years when we have hit our limits, but rather making pruning an embedded seasonal rhythm.

In horticulture, the timing of pruning is very deliberate and responsive to the specific needs and circumstances of a plant. For example, a deciduous tree whose leaves fall off annually has different pruning rhythms to an evergreen tree, and the best time to prune fruiting plants can depend on when and how they bear fruit. This variation even applies within a particular species of plant, with some raspberries bearing fruit on newly grown branches, and others on year-old growth, which means they require differing pruning rhythms.

Similarly individuals, teams, schools and systems all have their own particular rhythms and needs that vary over time. Even within the same school, differing roles will have a different ebb and flow over the terms or seasons. Therefore, the ideal time for you to step back and consider the big picture of your work may be completely different for someone else. We need to be wise and align with the pruning seasons that make most sense for the work we are doing. The key is to unlock the regular and habitual way of working that fits with the natural rhythms and cadence of school life.

Seasonal thinking

The seasons of the year are a central focus of pruning, particularly for deciduous plants. Similarly, schools have a seasonal nature, which impacts on when and how we might prune. It's important that, whether it's at the personal, team, project, organisational or system level, we understand what our best pruning rhythms are, and are conscious about setting them up.

Table 2.1: Aligning pruning with educational seasonal rhythms

Major pruning	Late winter to early spring is an ideal time to undertake significant pruning, after the harshness of winter is mostly past and before the plant puts lots of energy into new growth.
	This is similar to the lead-up to the end of the school year, or ahead of a significant mid-year break, as we look at what has happened, reflect on what is and isn't working, and start to set the scene for the year ahead.

Light targeted pruning	Summer pruning is usually relatively light and quite selective, looking to optimise the growth of the plant. At this time of year, the plant is surging full speed ahead with fruit production. Similarly, the start of the school year or of a new term is a time when everyone surges ahead. This is a good time to check in on things and prune lightly where needed to keep on track – but it's not the time to take out the chainsaw.
Avoid pruning	There are also times when it is best to put the tools away altogether! Autumn pruning can leave plants vulnerable to the elements over winter and is best avoided. In schools, there are times when, while it may be possible to prune, it's not advisable. These might be the times of the year when there are many events or transitions happening, when pruning would be too disruptive. There may be time to get into some pruning, but there may not be enough time and headspace for everyone to be engaged in the process to ensure its success. Initiating pruning processes may result in people venting their frustrations about particularly challenging tasks in the moment, but not having the bandwidth to move through a thoughtful and intentional process.

IN SUMMARY

- The horticultural concept of pruning has broader application to those of us working in education, as a way of helping us realise the power of doing fewer things, better.
- It is a fundamental flip in logic that to do less is to achieve more in the long run.
- Applying the Pruning Principle involves understanding the three key underlying mechanisms of pruning, plus adopting new mindsets around where we focus our time.
- First, pruning *redirects* finite energy and resources, giving the best chance possible for healthy, productive growth.
- Second, pruning *stimulates* desired new growth – by carefully selecting the growth that we stimulate through pruning, we can increase both the quantity and quality of fruit produced.
- Third, pruning *reshapes* for health and longevity – the strategic decisions we make to cut off or cut back help us to produce the best possible future outcome.
- Pruning can be applied at different levels of focus, from our personal workload all the way up to system level.
- Timing is key – we need to align our pruning with what best fits with the natural rhythms of school life.
- Work with the seasons of school – carefully consider the best times for major pruning versus light targeted pruning, or when to avoid pruning altogether.

ON REFLECTION

- How intuitive does the concept of pruning your workload feel to you? Do you experience some initial dissonance around the concept of doing less to achieve more?

- Did you initially conflate the idea of pruning with a reduction in resources? How are you now thinking about it?

- Have you already begun thinking of scenarios where the analogies of the three mechanisms might apply to projects you're working on? For example, where could you better direct energy or resources, or give something more focus to allow it a better chance of thriving into the future?

- Where might be the most fertile ground for you to focus your pruning attention on – is it at the personal, team, project, organisational or system level?

- Have a think about some current projects – what would be the most natural timing over the term or year for pruning?

- Similarly, what are the times in your school year when it wouldn't be prudent or wise to prune?

CHAPTER 3
THE PRUNING CYCLE

Understanding the positive potential of the Pruning Principle is one thing. But now it's time to learn the processes and steps that can help us master the craft. Pruning is not simply about cutting. It is best enacted through a deliberate and thoughtfully phased approach. Here we outline a three-step pruning cycle, which has steps you can follow within each phase. It's important to note up front that these are guidelines to use if helpful, but through trial and error you'll find an approach that works best for your context. See these less as inflexible rules and more as guidelines to follow for as long as they are helpful. So let's get into it – how do we actually go about the pruning process individually and collectively?

Figure 3.1: The pruning cycle

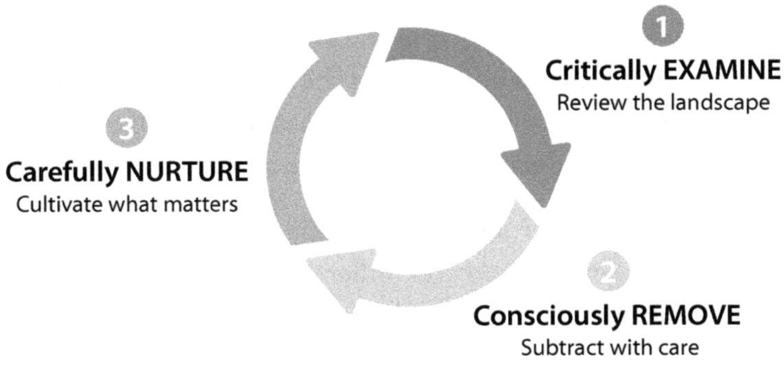

1 **Critically EXAMINE**
Review the landscape

2 **Consciously REMOVE**
Subtract with care

3 **Carefully NURTURE**
Cultivate what matters

3.1 Unpacking the three phases

In this chapter we unpack an adaptable three-phase Pruning Cycle that can help us work through a regular pruning rhythm (see Figure 3.1). Each of the three phases of the cycle helps individuals and teams to engage in a core element of intentional pruning.

- **Pruning Phase 1: Critically Examine.** Effective pruning needs to begin with a thoughtful review of the current landscape and then move through identifying, categorising and prioritising pruning targets. At the core of this analysis is the view that everything that is currently happening already has an impact-to-effort ratio: that is, how much impact you're getting from the effort and investment being put in. When working to come up with pruning targets, we need to put on our impact-to-effort glasses and see everything through that lens.

  During this phase, no final decisions need to be made, and no cutting is allowed. Your goal is simply to generate options for pruning and move yourself or your team through a process of explicit thinking about the potential benefits, difficulties and opportunities each pruning target would present. The phase ends by generating a rank-ordered list of potential pruning options to implement over different time horizons.

- **Pruning Phase 2: Consciously Remove.** Pruning in education must consider the humans involved and the relational and organisational dynamics that will play out. This means we must learn how to subtract with care. Attuning to the people and organisational readiness is vital here, along with being thoughtful in how we communicate and steward the change. Phase 2 requires us to activate our subtractive change management skills, focusing on the human side of pruning work in education.

- **Pruning Phase 3: Carefully Nurture.** This is the phase that is most commonly overlooked and under-prioritised. The benefits of pruning come from having a solid commitment to cultivating what matters. Here, as "pruners", our goal is to protect the space that we have worked so hard to create and avoid additional things rising up that would risk rapidly re-creating a similar state of overload. Pruners also fertilise and actively champion the things they have prioritised while collecting feedback and evidence about the change. They use this evidence to evaluate the effectiveness of the pruning action and make the case for engaging in further pruning in the future.

We conceptualise – and recommend – pruning as an ongoing and regular process. The Pruning Cycle, by its very nature, should repeat; completion of Phase 3 (Nurture) will naturally result in another opportunity in the future to re-engage in Phase 1 (Examine) when the next appropriate pruning season comes around.

The cycle is versatile and holds up across any level of use – from personal or team pruning, through to organisation-wide and even education-system-wide pruning. We hope it gives you and your colleagues a shared way of working through the process of strategic subtraction.

Sometimes you might be able to just pick a clear top pruning priority at this point and proceed with it without needing further prioritisation – particularly if it's a fairly standalone piece and isn't tied together with a raft of other interdependencies. In other circumstances, though, you may need to put more effort into exploring options, ranking them and choosing what to prioritise.

3.2 Unpacking the guidance steps

The three phases of the Pruning Cycle are broken down into some suggested steps to best facilitate pruning conversations and actions (see Table 3.1). As discussed earlier, these steps should be seen as optional guidance – not all steps will be relevant to all pruning work. As you and your team build a deeper understanding of the phases and steps, you should feel confident to adapt and adjust the language or steps in the model in a way that best fits your context.

Table 3.1: The steps within each phase of the Pruning Cycle

	Phase		
	1. Critically Examine	2. Consciously Remove	3. Carefully Nurture
Step 1	Identify pruning targets	Attune to people and environment	Protect the space
Step 2	Categorise pruning options	Communicate the narrative	Fertilise and champion
Step 3	Prioritise pruning decision	Steward the change	Seek feedback and monitor impact

The pruning steps and tools used will look different depending on what you are focusing on and who you are working with. Sometimes you may be working with just one other colleague or a small team to prune a particular area. Other times you'll be actively seeking perspectives from all staff, or the broader school community. You should feel confident to only activate the steps that make sense to you, while keeping true to the broader Examine, Remove and Nurture phases.

To download the Pruning Cycle and associated steps and tools in your setting, go to **https://pruningprinciple.com**

3.3 Initiating a Pruning Cycle

Pruning is best done with a clear focus and scope in mind. Before engaging in the Pruning Cycle, you and your colleagues will need to determine the specific focus of your pruning work. Being clear about scope helps you to limit the landscape you will be assessing. Will you be working at an individual, team, organisation, network or full-system level? Is there a specific domain area, initiative, program or project that you will be focusing on?

Wherever possible, it will be helpful to focus your pruning at a level where you have a direct influence or have been asked to provide input as a key stakeholder to someone who does have direct influence and decision-making responsibilities.

3.4 Pruning Phase 1: Critically Examine

Review the landscape

The first phase of the Pruning Cycle is critically examining what is and is not working, so you can decide where best to direct your pruning efforts. Think of this phase as like an orchardist carefully inspecting a branch or tree from different angles to identify any potential areas that may benefit from pruning, and then making a priority list of what is most important to prune now. The end goal of the phase is to have a list of prioritised pruning targets that you could take action on through Phase 2.

The following pointers can help you to stay on track through the Examine phase:

- **Examine holistically:** Look at both the detail and the big picture in deciding what to do and when. You don't just prune a single tree, you prune the orchard, and you also prune it in the context of the neighbouring trees.
- **Retain objectivity:** Try to aim for a state of detachment and rational objectivity in the process. Remain neutral rather than emotionally invested, so that you can be as objective as possible about each task as you analyse it. We must release ourselves from sunk costs and be open to the analysis landing wherever it does.
- **Get options onto the table:** Your job at this stage is to be as expansive as possible, avoiding making any premature decisions about whether or not the activity should be pruned. It is important to look at all activities, from the big to the small. Remember, the goal here is generating options. If we feel pressured into thinking that adding a potential pruning target will require us to act, we may limit the conversation and close down the analysis prematurely.

During the Examine phase, pruners work through a short sequence of analytical steps:

1. Identify pruning targets
2. Categorise pruning options
3. Prioritise pruning decisions.

Step 1: Identify pruning targets

The goal here is to generate a list of potential targets for pruning within the focus and scope you've identified – for example, reporting practices across the whole school. There are multiple ways you could do this, harnessing different tools and differing levels of analysis. Most approaches taken to this fall into two main pathways: the direct path and the systematic path.

For some pruning processes, participants may take the direct path – jumping straight to offering suggestions for pruning targets based on what is top of mind from their own experiences. Other pruning focus areas might best harness what we call the systematic path – which involves engaging in a comprehensive analysis of the entire landscape of activities happening in the chosen area before moving into the generation of specific pruning targets.

Figure 3.2: The direct path and the systematic path

Direct path
Straight to targets

- Identify targets
- Prioritise
- Prune

Systematic path
Comprehensive analysis

- Choose focus area
- Scan whole landscape
- Apply impact–effort lens
- Prioritise
- Prune

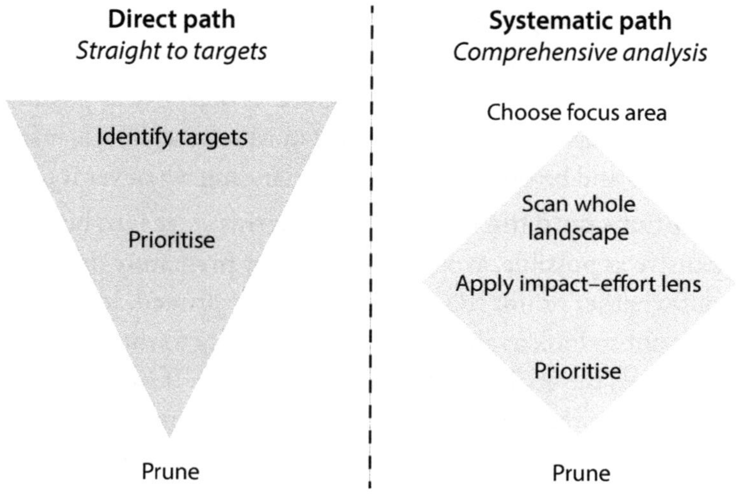

Direct path: Jumping straight to generating pruning targets

The direct path is a faster way in and a great place to start when building your initial pruning practices. This direct route can be helpful in rapidly getting people generating ideas for beneficial subtractive change. Embedded within these suggestions will be people's intuitive sense of things that are low in effectiveness or efficiency. It will also rapidly surface areas where people feel activities carry a perceived high burden of effort. As a consequence, this direct path approach may be how you start out on your pruning journey, working to build up a pruning culture by examining the targets that are front of mind.

You can structure a process for generating pruning targets within a pair, group or full staff – capturing each on a separate card or Post-it, or using a digital whiteboard or collaborative document. You could use simple categories for this, such as generating targets to "cut back", "cut off" or "cherish". Or you might use horticultural pruning categories such as "dead", "diseased", "damaged" or "problematic".

Sometimes, further discussion will be required to reach the precision you need on what a target is or why it is being put up for pruning. If you are running on a tight timeframe or want to help get the process started, you could generate a prepared list of potential pruning targets and then ask the group to add anything they feel is missing. This can provide useful examples of what you mean by pruning targets, and building momentum in the process will help teams to move more quickly into discussing this first step.

Systematic path: Comprehensive review of the landscape of activities

Other pruning processes will benefit from a slightly slower approach that begins by laying out the landscape of all of the current activities, programs and initiatives that sit within the focus area you've decided to work on. This is the time to get everything on the table – not just what people think should be cut, but everything currently happening in the focus area. This approach is more comprehensive and useful when you are doing a periodic review of a particular area of activity in your school (e.g. professional development processes, or strategies to enhance student behaviour and wellbeing).

When taking a systematic path to generating targets, the group would then work through a set of thinking frames, potentially supported by some tools, to help map out the relative impact and effort of each of the items they identify. It's a great way to dive into the whole concept of redirecting energy and resources to the things that most deserve it, as opposed to those that are "nice to have".

This approach provides a robust basis for making decisions based on evidence[1] and collective experiences. While it's more time-consuming, this method can be particularly effective once you have begun embedding a pruning culture in your setting and are looking to go deeper into the process to maximise effectiveness and efficiency.

> You can find a curated list of tools that support teams to engage in the Critically Examine phase at **https://pruningprinciple.com**

Tag the relative size of the pruning target

As you brainstorm pruning targets, you'll likely notice that they vary significantly in scale – some may be small (like a stem); others may be very large (a large branch or even trunk). Taking a chainsaw to school-wide PLC structure is much larger than using the secateurs to cut back on a few hours of activity from one instructional coach. Don't be distracted by size at this stage – instead, decide how best to tag each pruning target with some indication of its relative scale. This can be as simple as adding a brief tag to each target or using cards or Post-it notes of different sizes. Keep in mind that it may be necessary to refocus during this tagging process – the scale here is not effort or impact, it is simply an indication of relative size.

Step 2: Categorise pruning options

Now that you've generated a range of potential pruning targets, the next step is to look at their characteristics and benefits so that you can

---

[1] See Appendix B for a detailed description of different forms of evidence that might be relevant to pruning decisions.

have an open dialogue about the relative merits of each. At this stage you are not making any final decisions about what will or will not be pruned, but rather looking at each target more closely through a series of lenses to help organise your thinking.

Using a thinking frame or tool can be helpful in structuring the comparative process. The pruning options map (Figure 3.3) maps the level of difficulty against the potential benefits. This requires weighting the various factors together:

- **Potential net benefit** draws on all of the benefits identified from taking a pruning action. Keep in mind that the level of benefit will depend on whether you are partially cutting back the target or completely cutting it off.
- **Level of perceived pruning difficulty** draws on our knowledge of a range of target characteristics that are likely to influence how hard it will be to prune in your context.

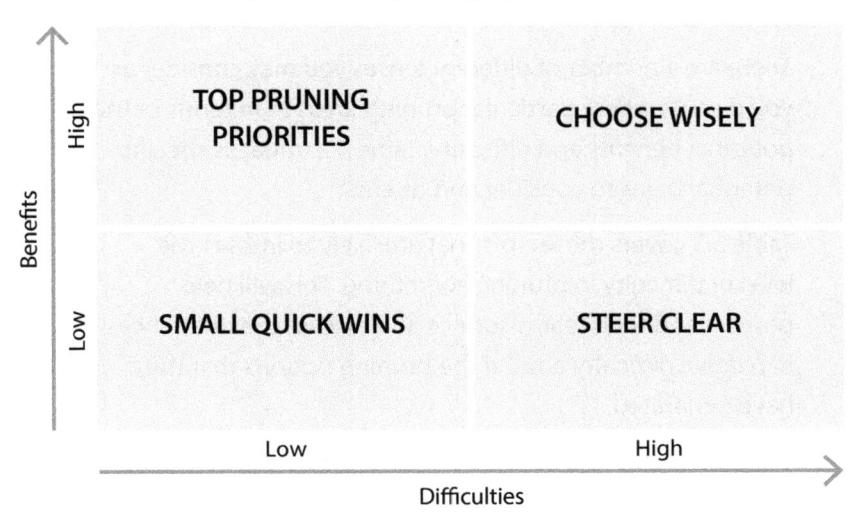

Figure 3.3: The pruning options map

Benefits	Low Difficulties	High Difficulties
High	TOP PRUNING PRIORITIES	CHOOSE WISELY
Low	SMALL QUICK WINS	STEER CLEAR

Mapping your targets out using this tool can help to decide where to focus your pruning – for example:

- Top pruning priorities (low-difficulty/high-benefit targets)
- Small quick wins (low-difficulty/low-benefit targets)

- Choose wisely (high-difficulty/high-benefit targets)
- Steer clear (high-difficulty/low-benefit targets)

Use best judgement to make comparisons

These factors can be relatively straightforward to capture but may be harder to compare between pruning targets. Take care not to get stuck on very granular comparisons here – applying your professional judgement and expertise and making general comparisons will suffice. You may well find that if you're doing the exercise in a group, not all of you are aligned on the potential benefit or perceived difficulty level of a particular pruning idea. You might find it helpful to get to whatever level of consensus you can for the sake of progressing the exercise (for example, take an old-fashioned vote!), and agree to revisit and decide on any trickier territory once the exercise is complete.

> **Going deeper on benefits and difficulties of pruning targets**
>
> There are a number of different lenses you may consider as you discuss where particular pruning ideas fit in terms of their potential benefits and difficulty. Table 3.2 unpacks specific potential gains to consider and discuss.
>
> Table 3.3 covers the factors that are likely to impact the level of difficulty in pruning something. This will help pruners and their teams surface and discuss the differences in relative difficulty among the pruning options that they have generated.
>
> Take care not to get lost in the weeds here (pun intended!). A broad sense of relative ratings is all that is needed. A number of example lenses you could apply are provided in the tables below – feel free to adapt these to your circumstances or add additional ones that are relevant to you.

Table 3.2: Potential pruning benefits

Characteristic	Measures	Considerations
Time	Collective hours of staff and student time	**How much time could we free up?** Approximate this by estimating how many hours you might save over a fixed period, such as a term, and multiplying this by how many staff or students this applies to.
Financial	Direct and indirect costs, including use of assets	**How much financial resource could we free up?** A general sense will suffice here – using readily available top-line figures from budgets, fees or similar. Indirect costs may be just ballpark estimates.
Human effort	People involved and the mental and physical effort	**How much could we reduce the direct and indirect human effort?** Beyond the time and money factors, try to quantify the human effort involved. Is this occupying a lot of people's headspace? Is it causing a lot of stress? Is it draining?
Outcomes	Impact on important outcomes	**How much could we improve specific outcomes that matter in our context?** The outcomes you focus on will vary with your target, context and priorities. Examples include student engagement, achievement, wellbeing and pathways or may relate more broadly to staff, parents or the broader school community. Focus on what you determine to be most important after applying your professional judgement.

Table 3.3: Characteristics influencing likely level of pruning difficulty

Characteristic	Measures	Considerations
Influence	Low Medium High	**What level of influence can you have over this pruning target?** Some targets may be harder to influence than others in your current context. It is important to capture this to inform where you put your efforts. Consider whether low-influence items need to be parked for later or taken off the table altogether.
Embeddedness in the school	Low Medium High	**How embedded is the target in school processes, practices and ways of working?** When a target is more "part of the furniture", it will take more effort to change. Consider where the target is integrated into processes, policies, procedures, practices, programs and ways of working.
Significance in school culture	Low Medium High	**Does the target occupy a significant place in the school culture?** Targets may be a significant part of the organisational cultural identity, making the change process much more involved. This could relate to their role in school rituals, their place in people's identity within the school, or connections to school history. Sometimes, this may relate to particular people or teams, and other times the entire staff or even students.
Appetite for change	Low Medium High	**Is there an appetite for changing this target?** Some targets may have very high staff support and enthusiasm for change, which can be good starting points. Others may require more delicate change management, and it might be better to revisit these once your school culture is more established in its pruning rhythm.

Step 3: Prioritise pruning decisions

The final step in this phase is to decide on your pruning priorities. You may well have identified many more pruning ideas than you need – this is where you draw it all together to choose what specifically you will do, and when. At this stage you don't yet need to take any action; it's about synthesising the thinking you've done so far into a codified list. This will give you the basis for stepping into Pruning Phase 2: Consciously Remove.

Make a call on priorities

It's time to choose. Use your analysis from the categorisation step to make a rough judgement about your suggested rank order for taking action on pruning options. Just make a back-of-the-envelope "good enough" decision, based on your current thinking and discussion. These decisions are not set in stone, and should be seen as a way of synthesising current thinking, not finalising.

Set time horizons

Drawing together our analysis and judgement, now it's time to rank in order the activities most suitable for pruning over both the "now" and "next" upcoming horizons. Consider the most appropriate timing for pruning a particular approach. Some things will be able to be changed quickly and with ease. Others might need more lead-in time owing to the complexities of the change, or owing to things that have already been set in motion for the term or year ahead. And some may need to be put on hold for reconsideration later.

The following categories can be helpful for prioritising your targets:

- **Now** – There are clear benefits and they are straightforward to change now.
- **Next** – There are clear benefits, but more time is required to engage in subtractive change.
- **On hold** – There are unclear benefits or the timing is not right.

> For pruning tools that can help provide a structure for ranking your priority targets in the now, next and on-hold categories, visit **https://pruningprinciple.com/tools**

3.5 Pruning Phase 2: Consciously Remove

Subtract with care

The second phase of the Pruning Cycle is consciously removing what we have identified as a priority for pruning. This is like an orchardist carefully selecting specific tools and using their knowledge and expertise to make the right cuts with the best possible technique. It is time to get those pruning tools out and begin to cut. Sometimes, this will look like thinning out and reshaping a project or activity in order to simplify and fortify the structural integrity of what we're doing. Other times, it will take a bold decision to cease a project, commitment or engagement altogether.

Some of the things that are particularly relevant for pruning are approaches to leading change, working with people, and implementation. Pruning may be new to you or your school; however, you likely have many relevant change management strategies in your toolset that you can use.

Step 1: Attune to people and environment

It's important to think about the nature of your pruning and any change management this decision may require across your system, school or team. Some things will be easier or harder to prune than others, depending on their level of embeddedness. You'll need to ask yourself:

- To what extent is this activity woven into the cultural rhythms and routines of the school?
- To what extent is it woven into the workflow routines and identity of practitioners?

Think too of the personal impact this may have on your team culture and morale. Will this pruning likely be perceived as a loss? Or might it be received with relief? It's important to actively try to step into the minds of your team members and think through what they may need throughout the process.

Take time to look at the broader environment. If people are in recovery mode, burnt out, or experiencing change fatigue, you may need to adapt how you approach pruning. This doesn't necessarily mean a decision to stop, but rather thinking very deliberately about the support people may need so that they can come on this journey with you. And keep in mind the time of the year and what that looks like in your setting. If everyone has just launched into a start-of-year sprint, they are less likely to embrace being asked to stop right there and change their practice. Similarly, you'll likely have some times in the year where everyone has run their race and just needs some cool-down time before engaging with something that requires change.

More broadly, keep in mind that stopping something established is often harder than starting something new. It requires unpicking it from embedded routines and letting go of the value it has been given. Attuning to people and the environment is the key to doing so consciously – and ultimately, successfully.

Step 2: Communicate the narrative

Communicate, communicate, communicate

Communication is central to pruning – and that's an understatement. Through the process of critically examining targets for pruning you will have engaged staff, and they will likely be somewhat (if not very) invested in the outcomes. Be sure to clearly communicate what has happened in this step, including: what was identified, how and why different options were prioritised, and what actions are planned and when. Take them on the journey with you so they have full context and can buy in to the decision.

The entire process is also an opportunity to communicate the rationale behind pruning, the potential benefits for the school, and how it will be supported and enabled going forwards. This not only helps to establish a positive culture around pruning, but also clearly communicates that this is not a one-off activity or "flash in the pan" that will not happen again.

How to language the change

In the technology world, there's a helpful phrase that's used when communicating about a program or feature that is ending or being discontinued. It's called "sunsetting". This is a great term to introduce in our school environments when communicating about upcoming projects or activities that are being pruned away. It lands more softly to say "We are sunsetting the numeracy project" rather than "We have decided to cut the numeracy project".

As we know, how we frame and language change is of utmost importance; there are very real human emotions involved, plus often significant institutional investment behind some of the things we may need to prune. Honouring what has been achieved in these areas and giving credit where it's due to those who have either initiated or been managing activities that are to be pruned is vital in order to bring people with you on the journey. Making connections to and honouring the past can be an important way of integrating changes into the fabric of school culture and the identity of your team.

Step 3: Steward the change

Effective pruning will require you to be an excellent steward of the change, carefully guiding the process. Pruning requires careful attention to the subtractive process in the medium term. We need to be on the lookout for any predictable or unexpected changes that may arise and make considered adjustments as needed.

Pacing the change

We recommend pacing the change that you put in place. After some initial success, we can be tempted to go straight from the secateurs to the chainsaw. Most gardeners can probably relate! There'll be situations where they lost sight of the plant and pruned a bit too hard. Some plants can cope with this and will bounce back, but for others this can be a major setback that limits their growth and fruit production for a number of years.

Effective pruning is measured and deliberative. This may mean starting with the areas of most urgency – such as diseased or damaged growth – and then prioritising what else is feasible. For a tree it may be okay to prune 25% of its growth back in one year, but for educational pruning we don't recommend going that hard and fast. Schools are large and complex human organisms – even a small prune can take effort to get right, but can yield significant benefits.

3.6 Pruning Phase 3: Carefully Nurture

Cultivate what matters

The last phase of the three-phase Pruning Cycle is carefully nurturing. This is where we focus on cultivating what we've chosen to keep doing, while also remembering to hold *space* where there used to be clutter. After we've cut back on some things and preserved others, there's a natural temptation to want to fill the space we've created by returning to the additive trap. "Oh good!" we think to ourselves. "Now that I have two fewer meetings per week and we've pruned away that extra event we were going to do, I have all this time to take on more things!" Or after three months of running a sharp and focused strategic plan, we start to add additional projects and initiatives because we are influenced by what others are doing around us.

The goal of Phase 3 is to deliberately and intentionally resist the urge to go back to our original workload, and honour the space we've created by following through on our commitment to doing fewer things – better. This artful balancing act of removal and preservation is crucial if we want our remaining activities to have the desired impact. In order for what remains to be fruitful, we must fertilise it and let it have the time and space to grow.

Step 1: Protect the space

To nurture what matters, we must hold the capacity. This means not filling up our agendas, to-do-lists, improvement plans or priorities back to where they were, thus using every single resource we have. It is counter-cultural to have "spare" capacity, but it is actually essential. Do you have some space at home that is often overflowing and a nightmare to actually use? Maybe it is a drawer, a linen cupboard, a shed, or even the glovebox of a car. Eventually, once it can no longer be closed or is completely unusable, you're "forced" to clean it out. Often that just involves rearranging things into a neater state, maybe getting rid of something, and then putting most of it back. And therein lies the problem with whatever the thing may be: it is still at capacity, which means it's on the verge of breaking point.

As it is uncommon to hold spare capacity, it is something you need to consciously maintain – and support others to do so as well. Part of this comes down to having and giving permission – explicitly telling yourself and others that it is absolutely okay, and even better, to hold your spare capacity. This shift may take some time to bed down. The gradual work of establishing a pruning culture can support this, normalising not only doing less, but keeping it that way.

Without care and attention, things can grow back in unintended ways. Plants can sprout growth below the graft that quickly draws away energy to grow a different plant – often with spikes and no fruit! Educational practices or programs that were once pruned back and primed for impact may veer off course, away from their core impact, taking valuable time and resources. This remains true for the best-intentioned and well-evidenced efforts. Therefore, we need to be diligent in our efforts to hold space, so that the thing we've pruned can really thrive.

Step 2: Fertilise and champion

We'll unlock the real benefits of pruning when we focus on actively fertilising and championing our pruning over time. This is how we make sure that we cultivate what matters.

Fertilising and championing the change also means ensuring that important needs are being met. We may prune to redirect resources, but sometimes we need to add some fertiliser too. Think about what you've pruned and how best to set it up for success. Does it need a bit more love and attention? What dedicated resources or structure might it need in order to grow (for example, a regular, dedicated check-in)? Does it need new rhythms or habits, or a well-timed deadline or horizon to aim for? Adding structure around what you've pruned is important in order to see it thrive.

Growth happens thanks to regular care and close attention to detail. As leaders, we don't need to be across the details of everything. But it is important that we find ways to keep our finger on the pulse, and consciously stay aware and in the know of what is happening in our classrooms, yards and staff rooms.

Step 3: Seek feedback and monitor

Finally, to nurture what matters most, we must put in place effective approaches to seeking feedback and monitoring. This is not about setting up onerous processes. Nor is it about collecting overwhelming volumes of data. Both are unlikely to hit the mark – indeed, you may have experienced the ineffectiveness of them. It is about having clear approaches in place.

Seeking feedback can be informal or formal – having open channels of communication is key. It is vital to ensure that those with a stake in the change have clear opportunities to provide feedback and can trust that it will be received and acted upon, and this information needs to be captured early and often. Simple pulse-check-style surveys using a short and clear rating scale can be quick and effective when combined with opportunities to also capture informal feedback via comments, discussion or feedback slips.

Obtaining timely feedback allows for adjustments and course corrections to keep things on track. It also provides vital opportunities to identify and celebrate successes – a vital component of building positive momentum around a change.

Monitoring is best done with a tight focus on key measures that can inform decision-making:

- **Progress** monitoring helps us to know how well we have done what we intended to do. Have we stopped the practice we wanted to stop? Is that always the case or only sometimes?
- **Impact** monitoring ensures we keep an eye on the ultimate objectives. Have we freed up resources to focus on what matters? Is that impacting outcomes as intended?

So that you can have confidence in any conclusions you draw from monitoring, ensure that you capture baseline information early in the process. Clear roles and responsibilities for who will capture and analyse data, as well as how and when it will be acted upon, help to ensure this process is followed through.

Across all of this, an eye for simplicity is key – we don't want the pruning process to consume any more resources than it has to. Where possible, reuse existing processes and systems, and capture only what you need.

IN SUMMARY

- We recommend starting with smaller pruning projects, where you have a high degree of agency and influence, while you get familiar with the process.
- The first step is to **critically examine** either the whole landscape of activity or, as a starting point, even just create your own list of pruning targets.
- The second step is to begin exercising your pruning muscle and **consciously remove** things.
- The third step is to **carefully nurture** what remains, resisting the urge to allow the space to fill up again and holding that space so that there's an additional spare margin.
- You must put in place ongoing monitoring in the medium term to stay attuned to how the change is landing and being implemented, adapting as you go.

ON REFLECTION

- What resonates with you most when you read through the educational Pruning Cycle?
- Where are the biggest opportunities for doing less to achieve more where you might unlock the most return?
- How might you find regular pruning rhythms in your role and organisation?

CHAPTER 4
PRUNING MINDSET SHIFTS

HOW WE WILL NEED TO CHANGE OUR THINKING

There are key mindset shifts that we are going to have to make to put pruning into action in education. As we've established, pruning in education is counter-cultural – it runs against the common approaches to leading school improvement completely. It's also counter to our human nature, with our wiring leading us to start by adding, not subtracting. So, while we may appreciate the potential of pruning, and understand how it can have an impact, we will need to confront and change our mindset before attempting pruning, or our wiring and habits will work against us, and we won't be able to bring ourselves to do it.

The heart of pruning involves a belief that both your long-term impact in your school and subjective wellbeing in your role will be improved through strategic subtraction. The inverse is also true: avoiding pruning in a feeble attempt to keep all our plates spinning will actually result in less long-term impact and personal and organisational vitality.

4.1 Shift 1: Learning that you can care by taking things away

As we start with our initial pruning conversations and experiments, we have a valuable opportunity to observe our own beliefs and feelings. For those of us with a strong belief that "caring more" equates to "doing more", a misplaced sense of guilt can spring up when starting to pare back your workload and cull seemingly worthwhile activities. This is normal.

It might be helpful to work through the pruning process with other colleagues so that you can reinforce the importance of this work and remind yourselves of the positive benefits and overall progress that will come with doing less.

We can also start to track the immediate benefits of reducing our overall load below 100% to a level that's more sustainable and achievable. Once we see this upside on impact and staff wellbeing, we can more easily upgrade our belief system to connect caring with subtraction.

The Pruning Principle is a liberating concept for many educators, because when we get stuck in the additive trap we feel that if we deeply care about outcomes for young people and about equity and inclusion, our only option is to continue all of the things we're currently doing while adding even more. It can be really hard to take out the tools and cut back a tree that we have planted, watered, fertilised and appreciated over many years. But it might be the most important thing for ensuring it has a healthy and productive future. The same is true of making changes in schools, particularly when stopping something that we, or our colleagues or predecessors, invested heavily in. How liberating it is to learn that the key to unlocking your growth is to do less – but better!

4.2 Shift 2: Don't be locked in by previous mistakes

Resist the temptation to protect things you have sunk investment into

We've all had an experience like this: A school signs up to an expensive three-year program with an external provider to run professional learning and support evidence-informed practice improvement.

It seems like it's run by a credible group, and other schools you know are signing up to do the same, giving you the confidence to jump in without necessarily doing your own deeper due diligence. One year in, things aren't going well. The presentations run by the consultants are long, boring and break all of the rules about effective teaching that they themselves are asking your teachers to follow. Feedback from teachers is that they don't find it relevant. Lesson observations show that there's almost no transfer into practice from the program, beyond your keenest group of teachers who've volunteered to be more deeply involved. The principal has now spent many thousands of dollars and 50% of an entire year's quota of professional learning time on this program.

Understanding the sunk cost fallacy and how it drives us

Enter what psychologists call "the sunk cost fallacy". We have an innate tendency as humans to defend our past investments. It is a well-established cognitive bias that leads us to want to continue with something, rather than prune it, because of how much time, money or energy we have already put in – even if it is ineffective, potentially redundant or no longer solving the problem (Arkes & Blumer, 1985; Kahneman, 2013). We simply can't bring ourselves to give it up.

The sunk cost fallacy comes up in many areas of life – a good example is a problematic second-hand car. While it may have looked fine upon purchase, it wound up in one breakdown after another, with you having to sink more and more cost into it. Rather than sell the car and start afresh, the natural human tendency is to continue pouring money in – not so much because we believe that the next fix-up will solve the problem, but because we feel as though we've spent so much money on it already that we're "too far in" to stop. The sunk cost fallacy prevents us from seeing all of that previous money spent on the dud car as a sunk cost – a cost that can't be returned, and therefore shouldn't be part of future decision-making. We get emotionally attached and hold on to things longer than we need to. Maybe you've had the experience of buying a piece of clothing online that didn't fit or didn't look good, but because you didn't return it on time or there was a no-returns policy, you've gotten stuck with something that you probably paid far too much money for but never wear.

Many people find themselves keeping that item year after year in their wardrobe like a sort of sartorial zombie. Even when we do a spring clean and the item gets brought out, still doesn't fit, and still doesn't look great, because of the sheer amount of money we spent on it, we put it back in the wardrobe. The sunk cost is already spent; you can't return it. Instead, we should probably say, "Thanks very much. I had to spend that money to learn that that type of clothing either doesn't look good on me or shouldn't be bought online."

In a similar way in our educational settings, all of us have a tendency to hold on to things that we've committed to in the past, that we've spent money on, and that we've asked our staff to spend significant professional learning and planning time on. It feels painful to prune them away, because we've already invested. Even if we're no longer convinced that the return relative to the effort is worth it, or that the problem we're solving is still relevant, we tend to get caught up in continuing things because of a level of guilt about what resources have already been "sunk". This can get in the way of effective pruning.

Releasing ourselves from sunk costs

So what is the solution? **Release ourselves from sunk costs, distil the lessons learned, and focus on maximising future impact.**

We need to be aware of this natural tendency as humans to avoid pruning because of a sunk cost, and once we're aware of it and talking openly with our colleagues about it, we need to learn to overcome it. We can't get back the money, time and energy we've put into things. However, we can think seriously about the additional money and time that we were going to add, and consider redirecting those resources into activities likely to have a better effort-to-impact outcome.

In our story earlier, the sunk cost fallacy would lead this principal to commit to the second year of the program and keep throwing "good money and time" after bad. But their alternative is to release themselves from the sunk cost. A Pruning Principle leader who is tuned in to the dangers of the sunk cost fallacy would move to cancel the contract, communicate the subtractive change narrative, and focus on how to use their professional learning budget, time and money on the best possible future impact next time around. They'd acknowledge that the money they've spent has taught them some valuable lessons about doing their own investigations, being more demanding about the quality of external PL provision in their school, and ensuring they set up regular feedback and debrief sessions early in the process, rather than questioning themselves and just hoping things will get better.

The moral of the story is: the fact that you've invested doesn't justify investing even more on something that's not having the best impact. Sometimes something will not work, or we will get it wrong, and that's okay. It's not about perfection, it's about the speed with which we accept and learn from a mistake and move forward. Focusing on the future – not trying to make up for the past – is the key. Nothing is wasted; some lessons are just more expensive than others!

Cognitive biases that can influence pruning

We need to be aware of cognitive biases, common to most humans, that can influence the way that we analyse impact and make pruning decisions.

- **The sunk cost fallacy** can take hold when we have invested a lot of time, money or energy into something and are hesitant to cut it back, even though it is apparent that it is not producing the desired outcome (Arkes & Blumer, 1985; Kahneman, 2013).
- **The optimism bias** can lead us to overestimate positive outcomes. If we don't have ways to look more closely, this can lead us to assume a positive impact without supporting evidence (Sharot, 2011; Weinstein, 1980).
- **The confirmation bias** arises when we tend to interpret things in a way that supports our beliefs and values (Wason, 1960). If we think a practice is "good", we will be more likely to see it as having a positive impact.
- **The status-quo bias** can lead us to choose to keep things as they are instead of initiating change (Samuelson & Zeckhauser, 1988).

- **The ostrich effect** arises when we ignore something that may be negative or unpleasant (Galai & Sade, 2005). This may lead us to ignore evidence that something that is "well liked" isn't having an impact.

All of us fall prey to these biases from time to time. So it's worth being aware of them as we go in, so we can actively work to prevent them from skewing our collective pruning work.

4.3 Shift 3: Every yes to something is an implicit no to something else

As we've already established, the reality of pruning is that it's about making trade-offs. We are working at our limits, and therefore trade-offs are unavoidable. But a crucial mindset shift we must embrace is being willing to actually *make* these trade-offs – in other words, to start cutting things. If we search ourselves, we probably still believe deep down that we can somehow "do it all" and that we don't need to make any trade-offs. We have to be conscious of this belief we hold, and challenge ourselves so that it doesn't get in the way of our pruning.

Becoming more conscious of impact versus effort

The best way to make these trade-offs is to embrace a different way of thinking about what has the most value. It's very tempting to allow "good things" that are consuming resources to continue, even if they aren't having much impact – because on the surface, they seem to have some benefit for "someone, somewhere" in our school. If you only look at "any impact", then you will want to keep almost everything! Most things in education have at least some impact for somebody, so we will struggle to make trade-offs if having any impact at all means something is kept, because almost everything we do has some benefit for somebody.

This is what we call "any benefit" thinking, and it often involves telling anecdotal stories about a certain student, teacher or team that is thriving with the approach, without looking at the broader pattern of how much effort it takes to produce that impact. To be effective at pruning, we need to **shift to a maximum impact-for-effort mindset** – where we get to know our impact and take action accordingly, being brutally honest with ourselves about which things deserve focus and attention and which are only resulting in small pockets of improvement or are merely "nice to have".

When we move to thinking about the impact versus effort of each thing we are doing, it sets us up for making the hard decisions. It forces us to get honest about not only the true impact of something, but how much effort and resource it takes to get to the benefit. We can then ask ourselves, "What could give us the most benefit for each additional dollar or allocation of time?" This process will obviously be uncomfortable. It will involve turning over stones and looking closely at the details of things that on the surface are valued and seen as good. But moving from just scanning to see if there is any impact, towards seeing all programs and initiatives through the lens of how much impact they have relative to the level of effort and investment, will fundamentally change how we view our activities. It will give us the courage to prune. The reality is that sometimes we must sacrifice "good" in order to get to great. Professor Dylan Wiliam captures the essence of this notion well:

> Most leaders try to improve schools by looking for unproductive things to stop doing. There aren't enough of them to make a difference. The essence of effective leadership is stopping teachers from doing good things, to give them more time to spend on even better things. (William, 2018)

IN SUMMARY

- There are key mindset shifts we are going to have to make before putting pruning into action in education. Otherwise our wiring and habits will work against us, and we won't be able to bring ourselves to prune.
- Shift 1 – we need to stop equating "caring more" with "doing more", and release ourselves from a false sense of guilt that to pare back on activity is to care less.
- Shift 2 – we must release ourselves from the sunk cost fallacy and resist the temptation to protect things we have previously sunk investment into.
- Shift 3 – we must consider the impact versus effort of each thing, and choose to cut back on some things that are good in order to redirect energy and resources to things that are greater.

ON REFLECTION

- Which of these mindset shifts do you sense are going to be the most difficult for you to unlearn?
- What are the areas where you are at most risk of "caring too much" and where you might benefit from pulling back on activity?
- Are there certain things that spring to mind when you consider the sunk cost fallacy? Where might you be holding on to something purely because of the previous resource invested?
- What are some things you can think of that are considered "good" but which might be distracting your energy and focus from things that would have even greater impact?

CHAPTER 5
RUNNING PRUNING EXPERIMENTS

It's best to pursue pruning through a series of iterative experiments. Here we can try out subtractive changes and notice both the impact on the outcomes we care about and the impact on the wellbeing of the people involved. Over time, this will help us build our pruning muscles and resolve.

5.1 Setting your experiments up for success

Pruning will take courage and creativity as we choose to cut back, remove and thin out for the sake of the long-term growth of our schools. We recommend running pruning experiments with smaller targets where you have a high degree of agency and influence while you get familiar with the process. Although it might be tempting to go rushing in, bright eyed, and armed with all of your new ideas, what's most important here is building early momentum and trust in the concept – for both yourself and your broader team. So how can you set yourself up for a successful experiment? Consider the following five insights from our experience as a starting point.

Insight 1: Build up over time

What we practise, we get good at. So start small, and build up your pruning muscles slowly with small projects. You may want to start by pruning your own work, practice and habits. Then build up to pruning with teams you work closely with, bringing others on board and establishing a pruning culture within the team. From there, you'll have momentum and some wins on the board and be ready to take it to a larger scale across the organisation. The more you take opportunities to unlock the benefits of strategic subtraction and do so in collaboration with others, the more you will build a pruning mindset in the culture of your school. As colleagues experience the positive effects of reduced workload and greater focus and impact, they are likely to want to proactively initiate their own pruning cycles.

Insight 2: Stay playful and curious

A key here is to not take yourself or the work too seriously. Approaching pruning as a series of experiments will encourage a much-needed sense of playfulness and curiosity. *I wonder what might happen if we cut back on XYZ? I wonder if we could enhance the zest and optimism of our people by reducing ABC? I'm interested to learn if we can achieve the same outcome by cutting back on two out of the five elements of our professional learning design?*

Insight 3: Take a manageable slice

As we begin to form this new pruning habit, it's important to address what gets in the way of doing it well. It would be easy to stare at the mountain of activity we're engaged in and not know where to begin. As the saying goes, "It's the fear of the mountain that will kill you". The key is to start small – think scissors, not a chainsaw.

For example, rather than trying to cut back heavy layers that might've been left for a long time by the leaders who've come before, it's better to build our pruning confidence and muscle by running some short and simple pruning experiments and getting moving with micro-actions. That way, when the time comes for bigger tools, we've got learnings and muscle that we'll bring to the approach. Don't try to prune reports; rather prune a slice of that broader challenge – the length and breadth of the final report comment. Don't try to prune the professional learning approach for an entire team; just prune back two of the five steps in the process that add unnecessary complexity. Don't prune all of your evidence-collection approaches for a school review, just pare back to the specific evidence types and examples that are needed to demonstrate changes in teaching and learning.

Insight 4: Find safe entry points

Pruning can meet with resistance and, at times, the change involved can be complex. So start at the other end of the scale at a safe and accessible entry point. Look for potential quick wins that are non-controversial and likely to be well-received by basically everyone. Avoid things that are intertwined with other practices and processes – rather, focus on what will be an easy change and will result in a sense of relief for the people involved. Once you have built your individual and collective pruning capacity and have successful pruning to draw upon, then look to take on the more challenging and complex targets that might require some more challenging stakeholder management to navigate.

> **Practitioner insight! Consider your choice of language**
>
> Language choice is vital in respectful change management, particularly when there is clear evidence to support pruning of an ineffective whole-school approach. Encouraging leaders to use softer terms like "reduce" and "shorten" has been essential to our success, making it easier for staff to lean into the idea of pruning. I intentionally avoided bold vocabulary like "stop" or "remove", knowing they may surface resistance and hinder productive discussions. By choosing less confrontational language, we achieved the same outcomes and gained staff buy-in.
>
> – Nicole West, (Principal in Western Australia)

Insight 5: Make reversible subtractive changes

Making large cuts that are hard or impossible to reverse should be delayed until we've built up some experience and a culture around pruning practices.

Pruning experiments can be reversible. You can say to yourself: "Well look, let's run this subtractive change to our personal or team routines for the next 2 months and see how it goes." At the end of that time period, you can review, reflect on the benefits and experiences, and then decide whether to embed the subtractive change permanently or revert back to your original overloaded way of working. Knowing that a return is possible often helps get our people (and ourselves!) over the line when we are first building our pruning muscles.

In a similar way, when we are doing a big clearout at home it is often difficult to make decisions to let go of some items that we know deep down need to go. Maybe it is a beloved set of kids' toys and books, or an item of clothing you haven't used for ages ("What if I suddenly decide to go for a hike for the first time in 15 years? Maybe I will need those boots!"). A good strategy is to put the items in a box or bag and then move them to a storage area in your house – perhaps the garage or attic or even the boot of your car. After a period of time, say a month or two, you can be prompted by a reminder in your calendar to make a decision about whether to go ahead with the giveaway or bring the items back into your life. This two-stage process can really help in unlocking some of the emotional baggage caught up in pruning decisions.

> **Pruning Cycle Planning Tool**
>
> The Pruning Cycle Planning Tool provides a structure for mapping out your steps as you work through a pruning experiment. Access the tool in Appendix D or go to **https://pruningprinciple.com/tools**

Areas to consider pruning

There are almost endless possibilities when it comes to pruning experiments. We've listed a set of areas to spark your inspiration in the table below. This is by no means an exhaustive list, but it might prompt your thinking as you explore your own context.

Which areas might provide opportunities to run small, safe and reversible pruning experiments in your context?

Table 5.1: Areas to consider for pruning

Area of practice	Examples
Operations, leadership and administration	
Administrative processes	e.g. purchasing, budget management, attendance tracking, room or facility booking, scheduling events, managing interruptions
Data	e.g. collection, analysis, monitoring, evaluation
Meetings	e.g. 1:1 meetings, team meetings, role- or responsibility-based meetings, leadership meetings, full staff meetings *See more in Chapter 7*
Personal workload and workflow	e.g. roles, areas of responsibility, projects, tasks or commitments, voluntary efforts, workflow *See more in Chapter 6*
Professional development	e.g. goal-setting processes, coaching and mentoring, PLCs and PLTs, action research and teaching sprints, observations, full staff days and workshops, programs, collaborative planning *See more in Chapter 8*
School improvement	e.g. priority improvement areas, key improvement strategies, initiatives, projects and programs, targets *See more in Chapter 9*
Structures and schedules	e.g. leadership structure and hierarchy, roles and positions of responsibility, structure of the day, time-tabling and blocking, home groups or houses, exams

Area of practice	Examples
Technology	e.g. computer hardware, projectors or interactive whiteboards, software used for learning and student management
Teaching and learning	
Assessment, reporting and feedback	e.g. formative assessment, continuous reporting, semester report comments, oral and written feedback, reporting cycles
Curriculum planning and resources	e.g. collaborative planning, documentation of scope and sequence, creation of resources, purchasing resources, textbooks
Domain-specific approaches	e.g. reading, writing, spelling, vocabulary, problem-solving, design thinking, competencies
Homework approaches	e.g. purpose, focus, timing and structure, expectations, communication with students and parents
Pedagogical and instructional practices	e.g. instructional model, shared or common practices
Student engagement and wellbeing	
Student support approaches	e.g. socio-emotional learning, tutoring, wellbeing, accessing external supports
Student engagement and behaviour approaches	e.g. systems and processes, belonging, attendance, positive/restorative behaviour
Broader school environment and programs	
Physical environment	e.g. wall or hall displays, facility use by external groups
Events and co-curricular	e.g. sports days, concerts and performances, open days, exam revision sessions, hosting external events
Transition activities	e.g. student transition days, data sharing

Practitioner insight! Getting started with pruning experiments

Just the data we use

We cut back our data collection to focus on quality analysis of the data we do have. This proved to be effective and useful. Having mountains of data wasn't helping to make better decisions, and the effort involved in processing and analysing it meant that it was not available in a timely manner. Cutting back required us to focus with more precision on what data was best available for informing our work. This not only saved a lot of resources, but also led to better and more timely decision-making.

–Nicole Jasinowicz (Educational leader in Australia)

Pruning reporting

With a progressive reporting system well established we reviewed our existing end-of-semester reports. Feedback from staff indicated that written comments in these reports were taking a lot of time and not necessarily of high value to students, parents and carers – so we considered cutting them out. We took the time to explore this carefully – ensuring everyone had a chance to have a say about the change. This was important as it identified that it was a high value to cut, but also highlighted what was necessary to make this change successful. As a result, we put in place a specific process for students who needed a commented report for a specific career pathway or transition process. And we coupled the reporting cycle with student progress interviews so discussion could provide additional feedback in place of the written comments.

– Michael Rosenbrock

Stopping learning management system (LMS) rollout

We cut back the rollout of a new learning management system (LMS), as we recognised that it was going to require an enormous investment of time for all staff across a number of years. While we had already started work on this, it was still better to change direction than persist. In the bigger picture this was a nice-to-have initiative that certainly would have yielded benefits but was not critical. We can consider returning to it once higher-priority areas have been addressed.

– Martha Goodridge-Kelly (Principal in Australia)

Reducing classroom interruptions

Interruptions to class time – be they loudspeaker announcements, excursions and incursions, sports carnivals, assemblies, NAPLAN, evacuation drills or other events – can take a significant toll over the course of a year. Where feasible, we took steps to cut back on these interruptions to reduce their impact on student learning. Some things, like announcements, could be stopped altogether unless urgent, or shifted to the start of break times. For events, we relied on prioritisation and scheduling – putting in place a process for booking interruptions in advance so that it was not a free-for-all. This also extended to balancing out the timing of any agreed interruptions – so that no particular timetable block was impacted more than others over the course of the year.

– Hayley Dureau (Assistant Principal in Australia)

IN SUMMARY

- Begin with targets where you have agency and influence.
- Start small (consider personal pruning as the easiest entry point).
- Build up over time, bringing others on board and establishing a pruning culture.
- Maintain a playful and curious approach.
- Take only one manageable slice at a time – start somewhere.
- Find safe entry points to get started where there is potential for quick easy wins.
- Make it reversible – start with changes that are temporary for a specific timeframe.

ON REFLECTION

- Where could you start your pruning experiments?
- Who might be most amenable to joining in during the early stages of your pruning journey?
- What would help you to take the first step and get started in one area?

PART 2

Pruning in Action

CHAPTER 6
PERSONAL PRUNING

TAMING WORKLOAD AND WORKFLOW

6.1 Proactively creating sustainable workflow

As you'll know from personal experience, there's no benefit in operating at the point where we're constantly overloaded and depleted. A crucial area to begin our pruning experiments is personal pruning, with a particular focus on our roles, responsibilities, commitments and workflow.

Too often, we are tempted to point our pruning energies towards external things beyond our own roles. This is understandable, because these larger things are often the culprits behind our frustrated conversations about what is going wrong. However, it's important for us to recognise that often these things are being driven by people above us in the hierarchy, and in many cases we can't directly influence them. This may make us feel like we have lost our agency in pruning, and is a thankless place to start.

Instead, we recommend beginning with our own backyard. Personal pruning is a fantastic place to begin, as it focuses us on the things that we can control, and involves making shifts that we will be able to feel swiftly in our own focus, impact and overall wellbeing. This sets us up for an early sense of momentum in pruning, and it's a rhythm we will want to continue permanently.

As educators, it is vital that we have some margin in the day. It's up to us to create more resilient systems within our workflow with some capacity left, so that we are free to respond to urgent situations and pursue new opportunities that might emerge. This means aiming to run at about 85–90% of our full capacity, instead of making the common error of trying to run at 105–120%. When we are functioning in an overloaded state, we will struggle to respond to new demands as they arise or to capitalise on new opportunities. Crucially, we also won't build in the necessary thinking time we need to do our jobs well. It's also, frankly, a horrible way to live out our work weeks, and the good news is that it's entirely possible to find ways to prune back and feel some almost immediate benefits.

Most leaders don't have a regular routine around considering what needs to be on their "stop doing" or "do not do" list. As our commitments and responsibilities pile up, it's possible to discover that we're spending all of our time meeting with others about the work, but not actually having any time left to progress the things that matter most. As we outlined in Chapter 1, this can feel like a state of frenzied stagnation. Greg McKeown, the author of the book *Essentialism*, suggests that the first thing we lose when we are overloaded is not the ability to do work but the capacity to prioritise (McKeown, 2014). From our coaching work with educational leaders, we know this to be true of many dedicated educators.

> **Practitioner insights!**
>
> **Releasing fear of missing out (FOMO)**
>
> I'm going to start pruning by reminding myself that just because something interests me, I don't need to be totally involved in it. I just don't have the time, so I need to learn to be comfortable with a little bit of FOMO (fear of missing out) and get on board with briefing decks and updates instead.
>
> *– Angela Dawson (Principal in Australia)*

Personal prioritisation

Middle leaders can face really tight workload pressures as they balance classroom teaching and leadership. I've found that personal prioritisation can be really important. Putting in place blackout times makes a big difference. Rather than starting with email or Teams messages in any "free" time and losing it all, it is better to disconnect from incoming messages and protect time for the work that is of the highest value.

– Leia Hands (Educational leader in Australia)

6.2 Run personal pruning experiments with regular rhythms

For many, personal pruning of just 3–5% can make a significant, perceptible difference to the experience of a working month. It may not seem like a lot, but pruning 5% of your time back over a 40-week school year amounts to two whole weeks saved! Some of us who have been running severely over capacity for a long time will need to work up to reducing by 5–20%. But this is best pursued through a series of smaller pruning experiments where you examine, remove and then nurture, getting used to flexing this new muscle.

Each personal pruning target you identify could become the basis of a short experiment, rather than a permanent commitment. Make a change, hold and nurture the space for 1–3 months, and then gauge the benefits.

It's worth noting too that personal pruning is not a one-and-done process. It's something that should be returned to regularly, with a rhythm in place so that it's automated. As you'll have noticed, roles, commitments and tasks can blow out again very quickly, especially if we are not vigilant through the Nurture phase of the pruning work. Many leaders find that implementing a light pruning rhythm every month or term, then a deeper prune at the end of each 6–12 month period, works well to stave off overload.

The great thing about starting with personal pruning experiments is that they will help create the mental bandwidth and pruning competency to later approach pruning at the team, organisation or even system level. It is very difficult to engage in higher-level pruning practices when you yourself are too overloaded and stretched. Furthermore, if you haven't built your own identity and efficacy in pruning at a personal level, overcoming the mindset shifts and encountering some trial and error, it will be difficult to go bigger. Facilitating or playing a role in pruning in a team will involve complex work and many stakeholders. It's best to start small, then scale.

6.3 Three-phase personal pruning cycle

Critical examination

Good pruning always starts with critical examination of the current landscape, starting with our own responsibilities, projects and tasks. For personal pruning, phase one is often best done with a review of our current calendar, to-do list, and portfolio of commitments.

When we look at our calendar over the past month, or even the previous term, we can see a story unfolding about what is really happening in our workflow and how we are structuring our time. We recommend systematically reviewing a recent work week and "reliving it in your mind" in order to notice and write down points of overwhelm, friction and extreme cognitive switching. Cognitive switching refers to the mental process of shifting from one task to another. Frequent switching between different task types and contexts can reduce efficiency and increase exhaustion due to the cognitive effort required to reorient attention and activate the relevant neural networks. As we do this systematic review of our typical workflow, we can start to consider how our various roles, responsibilities, commitments and projects are influencing our sense of sustainability and productivity.

We might also notice where we're taking on the responsibilities and tasks of others – saying yes to things when we really should be saying no – or where we're finding ourselves doing a lot of low-leverage work that isn't going to move the needle.

Generating and categorising pruning targets

From here we can begin to generate a list of potential personal pruning targets. These targets might include the following.

Table 6.1: Potential personal pruning targets

Personal pruning target	Description	Prompts and examples
Roles	Roles that you enact	e.g. team leader, literacy leader, instructional coach, pastoral care team member, mentor to new staff
Areas of responsibility	Specific areas that you are responsible for delivering	e.g. wellbeing, teaching and learning, programming, assessment, data analysis, allotments, timetabling, staffing, finance, regulatory compliance, staff development
Projects	Particular projects that you have taken on leadership of, or a particular component of	e.g. literacy across the curriculum, school-wide positive behaviour supports, tier 2 intervention support, high-ability practice, continuous reporting
Tasks or commitments	Certain actions that have landed on your to-do list	e.g. regular meetings, administration and compliance
Voluntary efforts	Optional roles and commitments you have taken on that are outside your core role	e.g. valued thought partner, advisory board, steering committee, external staff selection panels
Workflow	Prioritising, managing time, and processes	e.g. prioritising tasks, scheduling and calendar management, delegation

There are many different ways to capture pruning targets. In our coaching work, we've found the 3D Reset tool to be a helpful way of generating different types of pruning options:

- **Delay** – what could be pushed into the future to help reduce overload?
- **Delegate** – what could we empower someone else to do instead?
- **Dump** – what is not needed and could be stopped right now?

3D Reset tool

The 3D Reset tool can help you think about where you might be able to remove the excess from your workload by delaying, delegating or dumping. This can be used regularly to prune personal projects, or as part of a cyclical reflection on where your efforts are going. Some items you may be able to action immediately, such as stopping a voluntary commitment that isn't a high priority for you right now. For others, you may need to take some time to put things in place – such as building the capacity of someone else so you can effectively delegate a specific responsibility to them. You can add these to the "now" and "next" categories to spread out the suggested sequence of pruning actions.

	NOW		NEXT
Delay What could be pushed into the future to help reduce overload?	A1		A3
	A2		A4
Delegate What could we empower someone else to do?	B1		B3
	B2		B4
Dump What is not needed and could be stopped right now?	C1		C3
	C2		C4

Sequencing and prioritising for conscious removal

Once you've generated some pruning options and categorised them, it is time to consider the order of priority for removing them.

Now

Some actions can be taken relatively quickly – say within the next 1–4 weeks. Running quick pruning experiments – even if small – on these pruning options can help build a sense of agency while creating additional bandwidth to consider how to set up for other pruning options that would require further background work to pull off.

Next

At other times it will make more sense to take action at a later stage – in the next 2–6 months, for example. For some pruning options, it is simply easier to make the change if you set up the prune for the start of the next month, term, semester or year. A clean break can more easily open up a shift in your role, responsibility or commitments – for example, "I'll hand over responsibility for running the full-staff professional learning days from the start of the new calendar year" or "I will no longer be continuing with my voluntary role on a cross-school network committee from the start of the next term".

Sometimes it is easier to make a commitment to start the newly pruned approach at the beginning of the next month or term. This gives you time to work through the subtractive change with team members, renegotiate expectations with stakeholders, or block out the necessary time in your calendar. If you are drowning in work and feeling overloaded, you might be too buried to make a sudden change. But you can look ahead to a future horizon when you can make a more dramatic and long-term shift towards a sustainable workflow.

6.4 Building the capability and freeing bandwidth for delegation

For delegation, the pace of the subtraction change will depend on whether or not there is already somebody available who has the skill, will and available capacity to take on the responsibility. If you are in a situation where there is someone ready, willing and free to take it on, then go for it! At other times you may need to take weeks or months to free that person up (through running a 3D Reset with them to create bandwidth) and build their capacity and commitment to the activity. This longer-term subtractive work takes time, but will pay dividends for your future workload. Yes, it is often easier in the short term to just do it yourself, but this approach will merely lead to growing ineffectiveness and potential burnout.

6.5 Be disciplined about protecting the space

As the Pruning Cycle makes clear, we need to intentionally protect the space we create. It's the entire point of why we prune. This is particularly hard in the context of personal pruning, because doing this will reduce your to-do list, and it might even create a bit of additional bandwidth and time in your calendar. So often, when coaching leaders, we find that the guilt that comes with creating some space leads them to quite rapidly fill that space again with other people's priorities. A helpful frame here is in differentiating between *guilt* ("I am culpable for something and need to make amends") and *false guilt* ("I have a creeping sense that I am failing to meet someone's expectation of me"). It's important that we learn to discern between guilt and false guilt, and stop letting false guilt drive us. Nurturing free space and learning to say "no" is a crucial part of the Pruning Cycle. As the author and trust expert Rachel Botsman says, "saying no is the key to getting out of the cycle of unhealthy people-pleasing" (Botsman, 2023). It's not rude or selfish. Rather, it's about the confidence to set clear boundaries and expectations, which actually does wonders for trust. Botsman argues that setting clear boundaries and saying no with clarity is a trust-building move.

This nurturing part of the Pruning Cycle is particularly important in the context of education. We first need to create the space, and then hold it, to allow us to feel what it's actually like to work below full capacity. At first it will feel foreign to have the space and bandwidth to think creatively, focus on the core work, and turn up with energy – indulgent, even! Pruning our personal workflow is something that all of us will need to engage in on a regular basis; whether it's monthly or quarterly, you'll soon find multiple things creeping back in. Our job is to *examine*, *remove* and *nurture* regularly, and have support from others so that we can confidently make these decisions. The need for collective action here shouldn't be underestimated – pruning with a colleague or as a member of a team can make a real difference to our confidence and creativity in pruning.

6.6 Experiments to surface deeply held mindsets

Early pruning experiments are a great way to surface your deeper mindsets and beliefs. If you find it particularly difficult to generate any pruning options, or to follow through and take subtraction action on even the smallest options, or to nurture and protect the space you create, there's a story there. You have an opportunity to reflect and generate some deeper self-awareness. Be gentle with yourself, but also reflect on the pervading patterns that have taken root in your educational career and whether they are serving you.

You could ask yourself, and colleagues you are working with, some questions that open up further curiosity:

- What's driving my ongoing pattern of additive behaviour?
- When do I say yes when I really need to say no?
- When do I find myself stepping in and taking on other people's responsibilities?
- Why do I work hard to help other colleagues prune their workload while I struggle to give the same gift to myself?
- Why do I need to get to the point of total overload before feeling I have the emotional cover to say no?

6.7 Giving each other permission to prune

It's very difficult within a team or broader community of leaders to be the only one engaging in pruning. It can often feel as though we're the ones who care less about the work, or are less committed. But as we share our own stories of subtraction – of where we've dumped, delegated and delayed – and how we've held the space to focus on the things that matter most, we give others the confidence to do less, too. So often, we as leaders look to others for the right move and for how to do our jobs well. This regular sharing about subtraction and pruning gives others permission and freedom to do what they know they need to do but haven't previously felt they could give themselves licence to do.

> **Practitioner insight!**
>
> There is always more work that we can do in education – particularly as a school leader. After spending increasingly long days at school and noticing the early signs of burn-out, I've put in place boundaries and processes to prune back my on-site hours. I am at school from 8 am to 4 pm – in that time I am the embodiment of the school and it has my absolute focus. To make this work, I make a to-do list every day that I put into high-medium-low priority. Things can and do arise unexpectedly in school, but as long as I have all the high-priority items actioned by the end of the day, I can walk out the door knowing I have used my time well and done what matters most. I am now spending less hours at school each day but am more present around the school, more energised, and having greater impact.
>
> *– Daniel McMahon (Principal in Australia)*

Many committed educators struggle with giving themselves permission to engage in personal pruning. When coaching leaders, I've often found that the leaders who support their teams to sustainably manage their workload often do not give themselves licence to do the same. This connects to those pruning mindset shifts that highlight how critical it is to first convince ourselves that long-term vitality and impact comes from strategic subtraction. We find that many leaders who believe this is true for their staff and organisations don't apply it to their own work.

They feel that engaging in personal pruning is bad for optics – that it looks as though they're not carrying as much as they should, or that it will result in more overload for others.

To unlock yourself from this, we encourage you to engage in personal pruning processes in a pair, trio or small group of trusted colleagues you deeply respect. Pruning with other committed peers can help you to get unstuck from these limiting beliefs and give yourself what you need but are unwilling or currently unable to give yourself.

Recently, during a workshop for a cluster of high-performing primary schools, I ran a personal pruning process session. Everyone worked through Phase 1 of the cycle and had to develop 3–5 potential pruning targets – under the strict guidance that they needed only to generate the pruning options but did not have to act on any of them. They then each circled the pruning target that would give them the greatest sense of relief and renewed focus if they could enact it. In a circle, they each shared what it was, how it would help, and why they probably wouldn't be able to do it. One by one, I listened as their credible peers gave them licence and encouragement to move to Phase 2 – Consciously Remove – for the pruning options shared. The very things they initially struggled to give themselves permission to prune, suddenly transformed into wise and rational options once externalised and openly shared.

> **Practitioner insight! Email expectations**
>
> I have pruned my email use and supported the school to develop formal email protocols for staff, students and parents. I do not look at emails after 6 pm, and never on the weekend. I don't have my email on my phone, so I have to choose to engage with my email. My team appreciates that I don't place unreasonable demands on their time and students are also learning that teachers have lives beyond school!
>
> *– Dr Charlotte Forwood (School leader in Australia)*

TIPS FOR PERSONAL PRUNING

Review your calendar once a month	"Your calendar tells a story. Once a month, block out 20 minutes to review the month that was. Ask yourself, "If I keep deploying my time and energy in this way, will I make my highest possible contribution in my role? Where am I experiencing friction and frustration? What pruning targets would help me to get unlocked and enjoy more flow and impact?"
Actively prioritise your to-do lists	"A long list can just keep getting longer – and the most important items can get buried among the minutiae. Find a way that works for you to flag items based on priority – a simple high, medium or low is enough. Then you can prioritise acting on what matters most."
Say no earlier	"Don't wait until you are full. Start saying no and reducing your commitments when you are at 90% of capacity, rather than waiting till you are drowning at 120%."
You can't do it all	"If we dig into what motivates us, many of us who are attracted to education, and specifically educational leadership, are often motivated by the opportunity to do good things – indeed, to do many good things. But we can't do it all. And particularly, we can't do it all well. I've found reframing my thinking about this helpful. If I don't do it, someone else has the opportunity to. And if it doesn't happen because I said no, then it just isn't the right thing at the right time."
No prime time emails	"Even a quick skim of the subject lines of new unread items can derail us from using our prime time to get the most important things done. If it is an emergency, the first way of contacting you shouldn't be an email. Shut your emails when you need to focus, and find suitable low-times when you can respond."

Define your boundaries	"Be it responding to email or taking on an extra task – as teachers and school leaders, our boundaries can be very unclear and porous. It is all well and good to intend to have clearer boundaries, but if we don't define them and share them, nothing will change. So get clear about when you will respond to emails, or that a shut door means only come in if it is an emergency, or who is the go-to for certain issues. And of course, communicate that clearly, respectfully, repeatedly with those who need to know."
Go forward together	"It's really tough to make these changes on your own. Work with other committed peers when generating and acting on pruning targets. It can give you the motivation and permission to do what you know you need to, but often find difficult."

IN SUMMARY

- Personal pruning is an ideal place to begin building your understanding and practice of pruning.
- Running personal pruning experiments that save even just 1–3% of your workload can make a real difference to your sense of agency in your role.
- We recommend you do a critical examination of your calendar and to-do list to generate pruning targets.
- The categories of delay, delegate and dump can be helpful ways of considering pruning options.
- Conscious removal will involve considering when and how to make the change, and any capability development required for delegating effectively.
- Working together with peers can help provide motivation and permission to follow through on your personal pruning experiments. Sharing subtractive stories after pruning can inspire others to do the same in their own roles.

ON REFLECTION

- When have you experienced the benefits of subtractive change in the past?
- When can you schedule your first 3D Reset tool review?
- Who could you work together with to engage in personal pruning?
- What underlying mindsets might be getting in the way of your generating pruning options and taking actions?
- How might engaging in a regular personal pruning rhythm have a long-term impact on your effectiveness and satisfaction in your role?

CHAPTER 7
PRUNING MEETINGS

Pruning away at our meetings cadence is one of the easiest ways to start flexing our pruning muscles. By pruning meetings, we're going about a simple process of seeking to create more margin and unlock some compounding gains.

In our calendar, we need to examine a range of small-group, 1:1 and full-staff-level meetings and evaluate their effectiveness against the amount of time and energy we spend. We can then do the work of removing, where we eliminate or reduce the ineffective to stimulate fresh growth. Then comes the hard task of nurturing the space we've created – holding the line and ensuring that we nurture, focus on, and cultivate what's left rather than mindlessly letting things fill up again. Given the regularity of so many meetings in educational settings, the potential upside of pruning meetings is huge for most people.

7.1 Meetings meetings meetings

Meetings are part of the fabric of educational life. It really isn't a surprise that we're drowning in them. Educational work is human-centred work, so ongoing communication and alignment is crucial to ensure we are sharing necessary information and making collective decisions. Given that the adults in the building are often separated while working with learners for much of the day, there is little predictable opportunity to solve problems and meet on the run through the course of the day. Structured regular meetings of various types have become the default way of getting on the same page.

When done well, meetings can be a highly effective and efficient way of sharing information, making decisions and taking action. Yet over time, teams, schools and systems build up a legacy of default meetings that can diminish in purpose, effectiveness and efficiency. Enter the benefits of pruning.

There are endless funny memes about the frustration of meetings in education. For example (add the visual in your mind for each!):

- "I'm not sure if this is a meeting or a group of people just talking about stuff."
- "Trying to understand what this meeting is even about."
- "Wondering why this meeting couldn't have simply been an email."
- "When you're the first person to join the video call and wonder if you've got the right link."
- "When the staff meeting has run over, and somebody asks a detailed question relevant to just a few people."
- "When someone tells you it will be a 'quick meeting', but there is no agenda."

7.2 Huge potential gains

Pruning our meetings also pays back substantial, ongoing and compounding returns. If you could prune away just one hour per week of meetings, you would win back a full work week per year. I'll say that again: if you could win back 1–1.5 hours per week by pruning meetings across 40 weeks, that would add up to 40–60 hours. This means you have the ability to find an entire additional work week per year, simply by cutting down one hour of meetings per week. If you and a team of three other leaders or peers did this in your school, you would unlock an additional full month of time in the year! When applied to a staff of 40–50 that could equate to unlocking the time and energy of an additional full-time staff member.

There are many ways to get to that initial target of reducing meetings by an hour per week:

- Delete a single one-hour meeting.
- Collapse two one-hour 1:1 meetings.
- Reduce the default length of three meetings from 60 to 40 minutes.
- Change the cadence of a two-hour meeting from weekly to fortnightly.
- And many many more!

Sometimes this may realise even greater gains. The following table unpacks a few examples of potential time gains across individuals, teams and whole staff.

Table 7.1: Potential for unlocking time

Action	Scope	Unlocked time per year		
		Work hours*	Work days*	Annual FTE*
Cutting one hour per week of meetings	For you	40	5	
	For a team of 4	160	20	
	For a staff of 40	1600	200	1.0
Reducing the default length of two meetings per week from 60 minutes to 45 minutes	For you	20	2.5	
	For a team of 7	140	17.5	
	For a staff of 50	1000	125	0.6
Adding four meeting-free weeks across the year where 120 minutes of all staff meetings are cut	For each staff member	8	1	
	For a staff of 80	640	80	0.4
Changing the cadence of 60-minute all-staff meetings to fortnightly	For a staff of 64	1280	160	0.8

*For the purposes of these simple examples, the week is taken to be 40 work hours or 8 hours per day, and the year is assumed to be 40 weeks (200 working days). FTE is full-time equivalent staff; values have only been included when greater than 0.2 FTE.

How Shopify saved 322,000 hours by pruning their meetings

Let's call it a trend: many organisations both inside and outside of education are realising the power of pruning their meetings. Back in January 2023, for example, the team at e-commerce platform Shopify went through a major prune. They decided to kick off the new year by requesting that everyone completely revisit their calendar (McGregor, 2023). This began with holding a two-week cooling-off period for all scheduled recurring meetings involving three or more people, to work out whether each meeting was still needed. A two-week cooling-off enabled people to reflect on the real effectiveness of the meeting and to get out of the default commitment they were stuck in. In a memo, the Shopify COO said that the company would also reinstate meeting-free Wednesdays and limit large meetings with over 50 people to a six-hour window on Thursdays (McGregor, 2023). It's an amazing example of genuinely useful, intentional subtraction, with the intention of freeing up employee time. In total, Shopify deleted 322,000 hours of meetings (Hsu, 2023). There's a lot that we in education could learn from their example.

Cooling off

Why not consider a two-week cooling-off period where we examine what's really happening in our meetings? We can then decide on removing, and be very careful about only adding the things that have the most impact back into our calendars, seeking to either reduce or collapse meetings to be more effective. Of course, the goal of this is not purely to reduce or get rid of meetings. The goal is to win back time and mental energy to focus on the things that matter most. We're not anti-meeting; in fact, often a very effective and well-run person-to-person meeting can be the best way to progress the work. Such meetings are an efficient way to build trust, answer questions, and progress work quickly, rather than endless back-and-forth emails and unscheduled messages. However, pruning meetings allows us to rethink the default structure of meetings in our context.

Now that we can see the potential for pruning in meetings, let's apply the Examine, Remove and Nurture cycle to this area.

7.3 Critically Examine meetings

As always, we begin the pruning process by reviewing. For this context, we suggest listing our various meetings, their purposes, the time we spend, and a rating of their overall impact against their intention. The impact of a meeting will be related to the purpose: whether it is information sharing, alignment, decision-making, knowledge-building, accountability or something else. You could give a rough relative impact rating of one to five against the various areas.

Be as comprehensive as possible about the ongoing default meetings that are occurring. Consider:

- 1:1 meetings
- Team meetings
- Meetings based on specific roles and responsibilities
- Leadership meetings
- Full staff meetings.

Developing pruning targets

Once you've done a review of the meetings that are currently occurring, consider the following set of options for developing pruning targets. You might find the meeting-reduction map a helpful tool for structuring this process. Remember, at this stage you are generating pruning targets and considering the potential benefits. You are not required to act on anything yet.

Table 7.2: Potential meeting-pruning targets

Meeting-reduction category	Description	Prompts and examples
Delete	Remove from the calendar entirely.	**Not needed** Ghosts of past leaders and past projects. Meeting could be an email or briefing deck instead. The solution could be either removing yourself or deleting it for everyone.

Meeting-reduction category	Description	Prompts and examples
Collapse	Combine two low-leverage meetings	**Not the best use of time as it stands** Collapse where you can make connections. For example, combining 1:1 meetings to meet with two people in your team together instead.
Reduce default length	Reduce default meeting block time	**Embrace shorter slots** Change your meeting length from 60 minutes to 40 minutes, or from 30 minutes to 20 minutes. Implement quick "standups" where possible.
Change cadence	Shift the regularity with which it happens	**Space it out** Shift from daily to weekly, or weekly to monthly. This not only saves time, but can leave more space to do necessary work before meeting again.
Set blackout periods	Bring in a "no meetings" window where all scheduled meetings are paused	**Clear space where better use can be made of the time** This could be during intense work periods or low-capacity times, making space for deep work – e.g. block out hours in a day, a day of the week, or a week of the term. Put this in the calendar to protect the space.
Refine process and content	Refine what happens in your meetings for maximum utility	**Maximise the time** Refine meeting processes and content to ensure you are using that collective time efficiently.

Meeting-reduction category	Description	Prompts and examples
Own your calendar	Manage how and when other people add meetings to your schedule	**Don't let your calendar run away from you** Look at processes, expectations and culture for yourself and those you work with around scheduling meetings for and with others.

For each meeting-reduction option we can consider:

- How much time could we free up?
- How much of a perceived burden can we reduce?
- What will we lose by the change? How might we be able to mitigate this loss through other approaches?
- What more-important activities might get attention if we were to free up this time?

> **Meeting-reduction map**
>
> Visit **https://www.pruningprinciple.com/tools** to download the meeting-reduction map and run it with your team.

7.4 Consciously Remove: Cutting back and cutting off meetings

By this stage of the book, you have no doubt become accustomed to the human-centred work of the "consciously remove" phase of pruning. For reducing meetings, it is going to be crucial to tune into the environment and people as you make those changes, paying careful attention to how to communicate and steward the change. Obviously some people will be overjoyed and relieved that you are working to pare back meetings in the interest of effectiveness and efficiency. However, other people might have really felt valued through being a part of the meeting structure. That regular time with you or other team members may have been a way for them to feel seen and heard in their role. The removal of a 1:1 meeting or team engagement could be perceived as reduced access to or affirmation from you. For others, some of the meetings may represent a chance for social connection and feeling like they are part of something bigger.

And not to be too cynical, but let's be clear: some people like meeting and talking about the work, because it gives a perception of getting something done, while actually being a way of avoiding the hard work of getting the document, project or activity completed in the real world. It can be uncomfortable if that is taken away, and may be perceived as a loss – so pay attention to people's reactions and be prepared to respond accordingly.

7.5 Agree to run a meeting-reduction experiment

Setting up the change as an experiment can be a great way to help people open up to it. By explaining from the get-go that you're keen to trial and co-create the new rhythm together, there will be far less risk of a mixed response. Meeting members can be taken through the suggested change and reason for the shift (e.g. time and effort being saved). They can then come to an agreement to run that shift for a month or a term or even six months. At the end of that experiment period, the group can review what has been gained, and potentially lost, and then make a decision as to whether they should keep the pruned structure, tweak it, or even return to the previous defaults.

As always, running experiments is a great way to avoid the need to get everyone to have complete buy-in from the outset. Instead, run a time-bound experiment and see what is gained and what is "really lost". In our experience, people rarely decide to go back to defaults, but knowing it is an option can reduce the angst experienced by some at the outset. Once people have tasted more efficient, focused collaboration – not to mention the chance of winning back one or even two additional work weeks per year, just by removing an hour of meetings per week – they'll likely be very grateful for the upside of engaging in pruning.

Practitioner insight! Cut the information and focus on collaboration

In simple terms: if it works as an email, it doesn't need to be a meeting! We've cut back on meetings that just involve sharing information with staff. What matters most is using this time with everyone in the same space for priorities that require discussion and collaboration. This has also meant clearing space from what was meeting time and allocating it more specifically to professional learning and collaboration activities.

– Martha Goodridge-Kelly (Principal in Australia)

Tip from our team: Supporting the removal process to succeed

As a new middle leader, I noticed that certain meetings I was responsible for were not working and were dominated by administrative tasks – to the frustration of many, as this was valuable collaborative time. When cutting back, it was important to create an alternative way for the administrative work to be done. I used a combination of: a regular briefing email; some additional processes for making simple agreements; and delegation of responsibility for some decisions to individuals and small groups of staff. Just cutting back would have created unnecessary stress and likely a backlog of unresolved administration – consciously supporting the removal process helped it to be successful.

– Michael Rosenbrock

7.6 Carefully Nurture

As always, you will need to work hard to protect the space you've created through pruning meetings, and ensure that the time is reallocated to the highest-impact tasks for effectiveness or sustainability.

Tracking the upside you gain in time, effort and focus by gathering feedback from team members is crucial for building the case for sustaining and continuing the pruning practice. Be sure to celebrate these successes and use them to inform future rounds of pruning.

You should actively seek feedback about what has been lost such as: connection, alignment, feeling "in the loop", collective decision-making, etc., from the meeting-pruning process. Trade-offs will of course need to be made, but it will be worth being open to remedying any of these losses through other non-meeting activities. A well-crafted email or slide deck, or an open digital discussion thread for asynchronous contributions, can often replace the time spent in meetings, and if necessary, you can always reverse the extent of cutting back that was done (e.g. meeting length or cadence).

> **Practitioner insights!**
>
> **Refocusing meetings on impact**
>
> When I was in a role managing a team of education support staff, we had weekly meetings scheduled. These had been largely used for communication and administration that could have been an email. I deliberately cut back the number of whole-team meetings to fortnightly, and focused that valuable time together on sharing and building effective practice in our core focus area of supporting students in class. The extra time each fortnight was then used for 1:1 or smaller group discussions to support staff with their specific needs. It didn't save me time – but it freed up a lot of time for my team to do the work that matters most.
>
> – *Michelle Heintze-Moller (School leader in Australia)*

> **Enhance the meetings you keep**
>
> One successful strategy we've begun to adopt is a set structure for *how* we share information in our weekly leadership meeting. A simple four-question cycle to keep the conversations on track has been instrumental in being able to reduce meeting time and prioritise what information is shared in the most efficient way. Q1. What is your top focus at the moment? Q2. What challenge are you facing? Q3. What is your next best move? Q4. What else is on your radar?
>
> – Nicole West (Principal in Western Australia)

Fertilising and championing the meeting you keep: Enhancing the process and content

While there is much to gain from cutting back on how much time we spend in meetings, there is also the further potential to do better with what time we do invest in getting together. We can nurture this precious time we are investing in meeting by enhancing the detail of what we do.

- **Are processes efficient and effective?** More "useful" meeting time can be gained by improving processes. Can you cut back interruptions or hijacking of meetings? Do you need clearer start and end times that you stick to, to avoid time lost to waiting and spill over?
- **Is the content right?** Often we end up with what could be in the meeting, rather than what *should* be. Look closely at how meeting objectives, agendas and content are determined. Tightening this up to focus on what matters most can win back a lot of valuable collaborative time.
- **Are the right people in the room?** We're not advocating here for kicking the can down the road every time one person is away, but there is nothing so inefficient as having multiple smaller meetings on the same topic when you really need to get key people into the

same room. Or perhaps worse, requiring people to spend time in a meeting that is not particularly relevant to them.

- **Is the timing right?** Are you squeezing in meetings at times when few if any participants have the capacity to contribute in a way that makes it worthwhile? Consider blocking these times out and avoiding meeting then unless absolutely necessary.

> **Practitioner insight! Removing duplication and administration**
>
> Coming into a new role in a different school, I noticed that staff satisfaction with and engagement in many meetings was low. There was a lot of administration and a lot of duplication. This collaborative time together is so valuable – I wanted to raise the expectation of the quality of the work that happens in this space. The first step was to shift the focus away from administration by moving that information dissemination into emails and bulletins. This also reduced the duplication, with everyone getting the same information once.
>
> *– Justine Mackey (Principal in Australia)*

Owning your calendar: Hold the space!

Many in leadership roles may have experienced your calendar "getting away from you". Sometimes this is caused by commitments you have accepted. But it can also be caused by others being able to directly put meetings into your calendar. While at times this can be convenient and help make you accessible, it is worth looking at to see if you have the balance right. This is where we will need to actively hold the space once we have pruned back our meetings.

If others can add meetings directly to your calendar, consider making specific blocks of time available for this within the week. If someone manages your calendar for you, there may be value in working with them to protect specific times and look at ways to triage and adapt requests to prioritise what matters most and what is most likely to be effective. This extends beyond the personal, as it may apply to many in leadership roles in your setting. Look out for ways to build processes, culture and expectations that support everyone to control the overgrowth in their calendar.

> **Expert tip: Mastering the meeting schedule**
>
> Depending on your perspective, the whole-school meeting schedule may be either a thing of beauty or something that ranks up there with yard-duty allocations in terms of how contentious it is! I can highly recommend taking some time to reach agreement on key priorities for the year before starting on a meeting schedule. Learning as we often do through trial and error, I've found that this discussion is most effective when it's very grounded in reality: "So, we have 80 meetings to schedule for the year – how are we going to divide that time up among our key priorities and specific needs." If everything everyone wants can't fit in there, there are other ways and times to get important things done. It doesn't always have to be a meeting (particularly a whole-staff one).
>
> *– Michael Rosenbrock*

TIPS FOR PRUNING MEETINGS

Reset your defaults	"Our default settings can lock us into burning a lot of time on things that aren't the highest priority. Reset your defaults – be it meeting duration, cadence, content or composition – and pare it back to just what you need. I've found that shorter default meetings not only free up time; they also make us more focused on what matters most while we are together."
Create a structure that works for the core of your meetings	"Often we create meeting schedules that set out who, what, where and when, only to have to constantly adapt and adjust. This just eats up time – the wrong people are there, running over time, and late cancellations are messy. Spend some extra time on a regular basis getting key people together to nut out what you need most, who needs to be there, and how much time can be allocated. Then stick to it, unless something exceptional arises."
Cascade your content and people	"We've all been there – the first half of an all-hands staff meeting that is only relevant to 25% of the people there. Trust those you work with to use time wisely. If they don't need to know – let them go. And think about the order and timing to make this work best."
Keep it fit for purpose	"It could have been an email. I could read these slides myself. This is turning into a personal Q&A or airing of grievances. Our meetings don't have to be like this. Make sure they are fit for purpose. Cut out what could be an email, a briefing or just isn't right for the forum."

Protect your calendar	"It is a busy week, but you have prioritised well, and then someone adds a 2-hour 1:1 meeting to your calendar on an unclear topic. If you have been here once, you don't have to be again. Either through how your calendar is set up or the shared expectations you build with colleagues – don't let everyone manage your calendar."
Honour everyone's time	"Meetings can absorb so much discretionary time. I've found it helpful to keep a focus on the idea of honouring everyone's time. Returning to this idea when planning an agenda, sending out an invitation, or redirecting a request helps me to say no and only ask for what is essential."

IN SUMMARY

- Structured regular meetings have become the default way of getting on the same page, yet there are ways to refine and reduce these to gain more time back.
- Pruning back our meetings pays back substantial and compounding returns. If you could prune away just one hour per week of meetings, you would win back a full work week per year.
- There are many ways of reducing meetings by an hour per week, including deleting a single one-hour meeting, collapsing two meetings, or reducing the default length of meetings.
- Begin pruning your meetings with a comprehensive review of your current cadence.
- Consider where meetings could be refined, reduced or deleted.

- It will be important to attune with empathy to your team about how they feel about any significant changes to regular meetings, which in some cases may symbolise connection time or regular access to certain members of the team.
- Bring your team on the journey by reviewing and deciding on changes together, framing them as temporary, reversible experiments up front, which can be later reviewed.
- Once you've pruned, be vigilant about holding the space in your calendar for progressing important work, rather than allowing it to fill up again.

ON REFLECTION

- Where are there opportunities for you to engage in a prune of your meetings?
- Could you remove it or could you cut back? Could you bring in some meeting-free blackout periods?
- What meeting-reduction pruning experiments could you run?

CHAPTER 8
PRUNING PROFESSIONAL DEVELOPMENT

8.1 Enhancing the effectiveness of professional development

Professional development, which you might refer to by one of its alter egos – professional learning, teacher learning, continuous professional development, or staff development and training – is one of the most important levers for school improvement. We know that the most important factor influencing student learning is the level of teacher effectiveness, and high-quality professional development has the potential to lift the quality of teaching across a team, school or system. Professional development takes varying forms and is a common feature of educational plans for improvement – often seen as a key driver for developing the knowledge and skills necessary for delivering on a school's priority initiatives in the classroom. Every term, teachers come together with their colleagues to engage with evidence-informed ideas, collaborate and consider how to best enhance their practice.

Schools make a substantial investment in this space. Given the ongoing resource we put in professional development – both financially and in precious staff-collaboration time – it is vital that we regularly engage in a pruning cycle in order to revitalise our approaches and maximise the effectiveness of this work.

Professional development can have a significant impact, but unfortunately it often doesn't. This can be due to ineffective processes and routines used, and/or the non-evidence-based content that is delivered. A common gripe among educators is frustration with poor-quality professional learning, regarded as being a time waster that gets in the way of more-essential tasks like lesson preparation (Hunter et al., 2021).

Professional development is one of the areas where leaders can fall into a trap of thinking it can "do no harm", letting many ineffective approaches continue and roll over for another term or year. If a colleague wants to do a workshop for the staff on something they are passionate about, leaders think "Okay, why not squeeze that into the schedule". A team leader wants to send several staff to a conference in another city or state – "Sure, they are passionate about the program and it does relate broadly to our strategic priorities". Our teacher action research projects have been in place for a while now – "It isn't clear how people are specifically enhancing their classroom practice, but no one is complaining and we hope it's having an impact over time".

In short, professional development (PD) is ripe for pruning. Don't miss the opportunity to make this area as effective for your team as possible; it will pay dividends. We would recommend engaging in a PD pruning cycle at least once a year.

Table 8.1 outlines just some of the many different forms of professional learning across schools and systems that we work in, all of which might be appropriate targets for intentional pruning.

Table 8.1: Components of professional development to examine

Type of staff development	Description
Goal-setting processes	Formal school or system processes that support staff to set goals for their development, take action, and reflect on progress over time. This may include formal appraisal of performance in some contexts.

Type of staff development	Description
Coaching and mentoring	Supporting specific staff to develop particular knowledge and skills that are specific to a role, identified point of need, or career progression.
PLCs and PLTs	Professional learning communities and professional learning teams typically involve teachers developing their knowledge and skills by working in small groups with a particular focus area of teaching practice.
Action-research and teaching sprints	Teachers working through a shared process of engaging with research, applying it in their context, and gathering evidence of impact.
Observations	Learning directly from what is happening in the classroom to inform both individual development and whole-school approaches.
Full-staff days and workshops	One-off sessions and events providing formal professional development on specific topics or areas of practice. This can be external or internal, may be whole-school or for specific staff, and can form part of a longer-term series.
Programs	A systematic program run or facilitated by an external provider over a number of months or even years to embed a particular approach to teaching, learning or wellbeing.
Collaborative planning	Teachers working together to review data and plan effective teaching.

8.2 Keep the time and budget, upgrade or replace the process

When pruning PD, we need to approach it a little differently. We will rarely want to cut things off completely as we might with ineffective meetings or emails. This time is precious because, when done effectively, it is the single most important strategy for improving teacher expertise and thus student outcomes. So when we are pruning in this area, we don't want less of it, but rather we want to make what we have as effective and efficient as possible.

When pruning PD, our general advice is to aim to keep the time buckets and budget allocations that you have and re-allocate them to a more impactful approach. If you fall into the trap of pruning away the buckets of time, you will find it very difficult to win it back and secure staff buy-in for what they might then perceive as additional demands. If we let go of PD funds, we will struggle to gain new budget allocations in the future.

When looking for pruning targets in PD, you might consider where you can:

- **Cut back to revitalise** – Cut back on an approach that has been working well but has diminishing returns, has become overly complicated, or has lost energy and buy-in. This may involve cutting back on elements of the process, time allocation, who is involved, the amount of paperwork to complete, or any other design feature that is creating unnecessary complexity.
- **Cut off** a particular PD approach that is not fit for purpose and use the time and budget for something better. This could be because the original approach was not based on sound evidence, or was evidence-based but is just not working well in your context.

8.3 Sometimes pruning targets are obvious

At times it's easy to tell that a particular PD program or practice is a high priority for pruning. Maybe, like in the example above, you have had an externally sourced professional learning program that was consuming a lot of time and money and clearly was not hitting the mark based on extensive feedback. Basically everyone recognises this, and there would be no opposition to discontinuing it. That is pretty easy to cut, and that may be a good place to start generating PD pruning targets through what we called a direct path approach (see Chapter 3 for more detail).

Remember that when we make these PD pruning decisions, we want to be purposeful about reallocating the time and financial resources.

Example from the field: Pruning unclear classroom observation routines

In response to feedback from staff, we decided to look closer at classroom observations practice in my school. It quickly became clear why this was a lightning rod for frustration. Staff were confused about the purpose – was it a performance review, a chance to share good things, a way to help them get better, or simply a box-ticking compliance process? And there were a lot of different resources, protocols and terminology in place that had built up over time. While we recognised that observations could be valuable, at this point they needed to be cut right back and rebuilt with solid, clear foundations for effectiveness in the future. This was a clear cut to make – and freed up not just time but also a lot of headspace. These resources were redirected into other avenues of developing teacher practice – in particular the established professional learning communities.

– Michael Rosenbrock

8.4 Engaging in a broader examination of PD in play

At other times you will want to take the time to comprehensively examine the entire landscape of your professional learning activities and make relative judgements about their efficiency, effectiveness and vitality. You might have many approaches to staff development that are all doing "some good". In that case there is more work to be done in examining what is really happening by putting on our impact/effort glasses.

> **Practitioner insight! PLC ends via different means**
>
> There were a lot of things in place in our school to support staff development, including the recent addition of formal professional learning community (PLC) processes for all teaching staff. We realised that we were doing too much. The PLC work was not established or embedded and we were already achieving the same outcomes in other forms. So we cut back on the PLC form and kept the collaboration and support happening through established processes that were working well such as pedagogic coaching and teacher-reflection protocols.
>
> – Christine Lambrianidis (School leader in Australia)

Look closer at the detail

It is important to take a closer look to see what is and is not working well. Perhaps the content is suitable but the timing is wrong. Or the first part of a program was really valuable but the rest not really relevant to your context. Don't throw the baby out with the bath water!

On closer inspection, you may find that something has gone wrong in the implementation of an approach. Perhaps the purpose was not articulated – the case was not made for it being a good investment of staff effort. Maybe it isn't actually teacher development at all and is just information sharing and would be better treated as such. Or the details were lost along the way, leading to time and effort being focused in an unintended place.

Consider pruning the steps within a process

There may be opportunities to prune back part of an approach or a particular process or structure to make sure it is really hitting the mark. Be sure to get these examples on the table as well. For example, a peer-observation process that requires observation of entire lessons may be both impractical and resource intensive. A pruned-back observation for

5 minutes of a particular segment of a lesson could be a lot quicker and also a more targeted way to discover how to effectively improve practice.

Pruning the target people for each PD

It is also worth reflecting on how you decide who should participate in what. This most often comes to the surface with professional learning. While, yes, staff can express frustration about missing out on a particular professional learning – the more intense frustration comes from being required to spend time in professional learning that is not relevant. There is a lot of potential for freeing up time by better targeting development to the point of needs of staff. Of course there will still be mandated training, and whole-school professional learning to build common practices, but getting tighter and clearer on targeting can free up resources – not to mention keep morale high!

8.5 Examples of pruning professional development

In Table 8.2 we offer a range of examples of the types of actions leaders may take when pruning PD.

Table 8.2: Examples of PD pruning

PD category	Pruning to revitalise learning and reallocate resources
Coaching approach	The general coaching approach you have in place which focuses on broad individual goals is removed, so that you can replace it with an evidence-informed approach to instructional coaching within the same blocks.
PLC/PLT inquiry process	The PLC inquiry process is too long, and many people never get around to changing practice. You've known this for a while. Feedback has been clear that people lose focus and momentum. You keep the PLC time allocation, but remove the current eight-step inquiry cycle and move towards a three-phase deliberate practice approach that can be completed within a single term.

PD category	Pruning to revitalise learning and reallocate resources
All-staff PD day structure	The approach to the day has become a little tired and stale. You've typically had a member of the leadership team present research-based content aligned to the improvement direction. You plan to cut this back to a shorter 30-minute input and then create room to facilitate table discussion and group activities.
Peer lesson-observation process	This is running out of steam and not really having an impact on practice. After two years of encouraging peers to visit each other's classrooms once a term and follow a debrief and feedback protocol, you've achieved your goal of a new culture of openness. But now everyone just seems to be going through the motions. You decide to prune peer observations right back to the core and remove the current format. To align this effort better with staff development needs, you begin some trials of videoing lessons to find out what else could work well in your context.
External conference to external school visit	You've been sending a couple of people to an external training event that is unlikely to be transferred back into classroom practice. Instead, this time and budget could be allocated to those staff members spending 1–2 days shadowing practitioners in a school that has successfully implemented an approach your school is working on. This grounded learning is more likely to provide practical tools and guidance that could transfer back into the school.
Stopping expensive externally provided 3-year program	After 6 months, it is clear that an expensive multi-year pedagogical change program run by external consultants is not working. The PowerPoint workshops are overloaded with content, and little support is provided to enable teachers to implement effectively. The school decides to prune this provider and reallocate the resource to an internally driven agenda, utilising the expertise of two key literacy champions within their school. Some of the funding is then used to free up those champions to do some classroom-embedded instructional coaching and join co-planning sessions with teams of teachers.

8.6 Running your own Critically Examine phase of a PD-pruning cycle

Identify and capture what you do on separate Post-it notes or cards

The landscape of staff development looks different across schools and systems. There are many facets of programs, processes and culture that contribute to professional development, and these are often deeply interconnected.

It is important to get below the surface to understand the complete picture in your setting. This is the time to get everything on the table – not just the headline, but what it looks like in practice. So what might make up this picture?

A simple approach to getting everything you do on the table is to capture the what, who and when. This can be as simple as brainstorming onto Post-it notes or pre-printed cards. Alternatively, capturing inputs using an online survey tool works well. Keep in mind that this is just about finding a structured way to gather information.

What	Concise details of what it is. Note not just the form, but what capacity it aims to develop.
Who	The specific staff, teams or groupings involved. Note the approximate number of staff.
When	Timing within the week, term or year. Note the approximate number of hours per person across a relevant period.

For example, this could look like:

What	**Action research projects**
	Teacher practice-focused inquiry projects to identify a priority area to work on, engage with evidence, develop and trial a tight change to practice, and reflect on impact.
Who	All teaching staff in allocated groups of approximately three – 45 teachers in total.

| When | Every second Wednesday after school for an hour. Approximately 18 hours per year per staff member. Total of 810 staff hours over the year (100+ days). |

What	Instructional coaching
	Releasing expert teachers to provide targeted instructional coaching to specific staff focused on an identified point of need. Focus is granular changes to practice – refined and embedded.
Who	Two coaches working with 12 teaching staff in total.
When	Coaching cycle runs for one term. Each staff member allocated 5 hours of coaching covered with equivalent release from yard duty. Coach time is part of their allotment. Total of 120 hours per term, and 480 hours per year (60 days).

8.7 Categorise PD-pruning options

To be able to make effective pruning decisions, we need to apply different lenses to categorise the possible options.

Bring your effort–impact thinking to the table

This is the time to bring your effort–impact thinking to the table. What are all of the resources that we are putting into running this coaching program? How much load is the optional professional learning program putting on our teachers? Is our teachers' action-research process having an impact on classroom practice?

You could use the Pruning Matrix (See Appendix C) or another tool of choice to evaluate and visually categorise (visit https://pruningprinciple.com for a range of options).

Use the feedback you already have and welcome constructive input

What is the word on the ground about your staff development approaches? Staff development inherently involves many staff – so be sure to welcome constructive input as part of the pruning process.

This feedback can help to get more granular on the details of what is and isn't working.

Draw on knowledge of what can be effective

Where there is applicable research evidence, we can draw on this to help consider the effectiveness of different approaches. For example, there is a significant body of knowledge on what contributes to the effectiveness of professional learning. It has a better chance of being effective when it is embedded in a school and role, has leadership support, and is sustained over time (Cole, 2012; Cordingley et al., 2015; Timperley et al., 2007). The Education Endowment Foundation identified four key aspects that make it more likely to lead to more-effective professional development: building knowledge, motivating, developing techniques, and embedding practice (Education Endowment Foundation, 2021). If any of these are not present, which is typical in many one-off professional learning events, consider taking a close look at the details to see how much impact a particular approach to PD is having.

Consider alignment and connection

Staff development can be a lightning rod for frustration. It must be very clearly framed, have a well-understood purpose, be linked to the bigger-picture journey and priorities of the school, and have direct relevance to the core work of those involved. And rightly so – if it isn't aligned with school priorities or meeting specific needs of staff, it likely isn't a good use of finite resources. Consider this alignment with priorities and connection to core work when categorising targets.

Look at the bigger picture on timing and capacity

It is also worth considering how your staff development approaches align with the cycles of the school year in setting and teacher capacity. Teachers, like schools, have finite capacity. This is not just about workload but also about the effect of juggling many things at once – we can only keep juggling so many balls in the air effectively. Consider where you might be stretching things too thin. Does that professional learning session on something unrelated need to be run immediately before a parent–teacher conference evening? Should you keep running formal action inquiry projects for teachers in the same year that you are implementing a completely new curriculum? Will professional learning in the last few days of the school year translate well into improved practice when staff return after the break?

8.8 Prioritise your finite capacity for staff development

The next step in pruning is to prioritise what to prune and when – decision time. While sometimes the priorities may stand out like a sore thumb, pruning staff development commonly requires trade-offs. This can seem like making difficult decisions, but it's vital for prioritising capacity.

Finding a "good enough" balance

Taking a holistic approach is important for prioritising. Having looked at everything that you do and having unpacked the details of what it looks like in practice – is the overall balance right? This is about getting it good enough, not perfect. Have you got a balance between meeting individual staff development needs and working on whole-school priorities? What collaborative work is most valuable to staff and the school right now?

Time it right, start small

When you have some priorities to cut – be sure to consider timing. "The coaching program just isn't working, but we need to wait until the end of this coaching cycle before winding it up. We need to rethink our mentoring approach for early-career teachers when we plan for next year."

Consider starting small and simple to get some wins on the board. Maybe there are some quick wins in removing parts of a practice that are a good pruning target – such as removing administrative or communication items from agendas for professional learning time.

Or this can just be saying no to things that have not yet begun – such as not signing up to that additional professional learning program for next term.

Practitioner insights!

Embedding a shift from form to process

I noticed that the way professional learning communities (PLCs) were running was focused on the form – on it being something that we do. For it to have impact I knew it was important that it focused on effective processes – a way of working. So this was a priority to cut back and rejuvenate. The challenge was to do so in such a way that it didn't just end up reverting to the familiar. There were three keys to making this work: emphasising the importance of creating space and time for deep thinking together; refining roles so there was effective leadership and facilitation within PLCs; and putting in place support to build everyone's capacity to make the most of PLC time.

– Justine Mackey (Principal in Australia)

PD share-backs

We had in place a requirement for staff to share back what they had learned after attending external professional development. The intention was good but in practice it had become inefficient. It wasn't always relevant to everyone and was consuming a lot of collaborative time. So we cut this back and focused instead on supporting staff to identify on a case-by-case basis how and with whom they could do their PD share-back.

– Nicole Jasinowicz (School leader in Australia)

Asking important questions about staff development days

Whole staff development days can be a valuable opportunity for substantial efforts that involve everyone. However, it is often very contested terrain. It can seem like everyone is bidding for time on those days – to get some time with staff to do what they see as a priority. Teaching teams often want collaborative planning time together. And it can also be the best time to access an external PD provider. Put all this together and you can end up with a real mixed bag that pleases no one and doesn't use time well either. This can be a fruitful area to examine. Could the day have more impact if you agree to do less, but better? Is there a shared understanding of priorities for this precious time? Have you got the right balance among competing interests? What things could you efficiently and effectively shift elsewhere?

TIPS FOR PRUNING STAFF DEVELOPMENT

Stay focused on the core purpose	"We've probably all experienced an approach to professional learning or collaboration that has degraded into jumping through hoops or going through the motions – form over function – even with things that started out well. Always keep returning to the core purpose – developing staff capacity to work effectively together and improve student outcomes. If it doesn't do this job, either reform it, or stop doing it."

Watch out for sunk cost thinking	"You might have personally invested a lot of time, effort and capital into a PD program or approach – making the case to staff, lending it your credibility. And PD efforts are often very visible and involve most staff. But don't let that get in the way of seeing what isn't working and taking action. It is better to learn lessons early. Be prepared to cut your losses on sunk costs and stop what isn't working so you can use that resource for something better."
Find the right form	"We've cut back on forms of professional development that were just not working well, and done the same job in a different way. In particular, making some professional learning into self-directed modules has allowed staff to engage at a time and pace that works for them. It has also freed up valuable collaborative time and is reusable. It won't always be the right solution, but definitely consider when it is a good fit."

IN SUMMARY

- Staff development represents a significant investment from schools, and it is vital we regularly examine it to ensure it is effective.

- Sometimes a high priority for pruning development will be very clear, straightforward and well received.

- Further pruning of staff development is likely to involve trade-offs and exploration of how different approaches are interconnected.

- Bring your effort–impact lens to the table when categorising options.

- Draw on staff feedback and research evidence to build a clear picture of what is or is not working and why.

ON REFLECTION

- What is really moving the needle on teacher knowledge and practice change?

- Are there opportunities to prune back processes or parts of a staff development approach that are not having the impact they could have?

- Could you achieve a greater impact by cutting off one low-impact component of professional development and reallocating that time to a more effective PD design?

- How could your understanding of the effective characteristics of professional learning from the research help you to choose between various PD forms? (Education Endowment Foundation, 2021)

- Would tightening and clarifying who can or must participate in particular development activities free up resources and ensure that PD is targeted at the right people?

CHAPTER 9
PRUNING IMPROVEMENT PLANS

9.1 The pitfalls of overloaded plans

When considering educational pruning, one of the most important areas of focus is that of improvement priorities and plans. Annual improvement plans, at times nested within a broader 3–4-year strategic plan, are followed by most teams, schools and systems we work in. The stated intent of these plans is to make clear decisions about which areas of improvement we will prioritise, outlining the implementation strategies that will get us there and mapping out the evidence that will help us determine if we are making progress towards our planned goals. Strategic improvement planning should be about making hard and explicit decisions about what we will and will not deliberately improve over a certain period of time. As the strategist Professor Michael Porter from Harvard says, "the essence of strategy is choosing what not to do" (Porter, 1996). Indeed – strategy is what you say "no" to.

Unfortunately, the lived reality of educational improvement plans shows that these documents often end up completely overloaded and weighed down with unrealistic expectations. Even when planning templates suggest having a sharp and narrow focus on one to three priority areas, leaders often feel compelled to make those three areas broad themes instead – such as "teaching", "wellbeing" and "community" – under which they end up grouping the 17-plus activities and initiatives that they need to pursue. Suddenly, those one to three priority areas feel very blurry.

School and system improvement is hard and complex work, involving developing new capabilities, routines and cultures. It is almost impossible to improve more than a few things in any given year, and these often need to be implemented in a thoughtful and logical sequence that avoids overloading staff and resources. Our bloated and unrealistic improvement plans are becoming more of a hindrance than an enabler of sustainable improvement. We need to refine.

We are about to discover how pruning can help us make improvement planning a force for making meaningful progress together. It is a process that can help our plans become clear, simplified and realistic documents that can unite a team and staff around a collective improvement agenda.

9.2 Establishing a rhythm of pruning before planning

First, we want to suggest that the new order of operations for improvement planning should actually be subtraction before addition. Each year, teams gather to pull together an improvement plan for the year ahead. The problem is, these improvement conversations tend to assume that everything currently happening will continue, while new programs, initiatives and tasks are added on top of them.

As we have already established, we're already operating at full capacity, if not over capacity, in how we utilise our budgets, our human resources, and our time within our schools. Therefore, any attempts to do additional improvement planning without first engaging in subtraction is only going to result in overload or shallow and ineffective implementation. It's what we call *improvement theatre*, where people add the new language and pretend to make changes for a while, but don't go about the deep implementation that's necessary to achieve a real change in outcomes.

We need to establish a new rhythm in our organisations and teams where we engage in annual pruning before annual planning. Whether it's a month or two in front, or just a few days or weeks before we engage in any additive thinking, we first need to engage in the strategic subtraction that creates space for the work we're choosing to do. Indeed, we would go so far as to suggest that every school or district or system improvement planning template shouldn't just have an outline of the new goals and strategies that we're going to pursue, but should first have *a pruning box within the template*, outlining what the school is committing to stop doing this year.

> We need to establish a new rhythm in our organisations and teams where we engage in annual pruning before annual planning.

Sometimes, this pruning before our planning will involve stopping doing something or removing something to free up resources and bandwidth to be redeployed towards new priorities and initiatives. At other times, this pruning will identify that some programs and initiatives have been sufficiently rolled out and can now form part of the embedded practices, routines and rhythms of the team or organisation. This means these items can be pruned from the improvement agenda, as they're now business-as-usual. To be clear, these programs and initiatives are not being removed completely from the operations of the school, but are only being pruned from the explicit improvement agenda. They now move across into maintenance mode, rather than filling up a precious spot in the explicit improvement agenda.

The first way to apply pruning to our improvement priorities and plans is to ensure that we follow the rule of pruning (subtraction) before planning (addition).

9.3 How to prune your plan

There is substantial diversity in the structure and language used in educational improvement planning around the world. We all do it differently. We encourage you and your colleagues to look for creative ways to cut off, cut back, streamline, remove and refine each element of your plan until it looks feasible and clear.

The following table outlines a set of categories to get you started in exploring ways to prune your plan.

Table 9.1: Areas to examine when pruning improvement plans

Improvement plan area	Description	Prompts and examples
Priority improvement areas	Current priority focus areas	What is your best focus right now? Look beyond the number of areas to their relative size and the likely effort required to effect change in them.
Key improvement strategies	Vital levers for improvement in each area	What are the things you can focus your efforts on that are most likely to produce improvement in the priority areas in your context? Do you have too many on the go at the same time?
Initiatives, projects and programs	Specific actions that enact the strategies	Are these the most suitable initiatives? Are they sequenced in the right order? Is there capacity to implement them in the timeframes? Do you need to clear other things out of the way so these priority initiatives can be done well?
Targets	Ways of measuring progress and impact	Are the targets clearly aligned to the priority and relevant to your context? Where can you use existing data sources and feedback mechanisms? Have you got the balance right on collecting just enough information (rather than all the information) so that it is informative and actionable?

Having worked in multiple systems around the world, we know that many school leaders in particular feel locked in to compliance-based plans that cover almost every aspect of education, despite the fact that everyone knows they are unrealistic and that very little within the document will be implemented. In cases like these, we normally suggest that you complete your compliance plan to "keep the system happy" and then generate a more agile iterative plan as a flexible online document (e.g. Google Docs or OneNote) that succinctly captures your decisions about what you are "really" committing to completing this year.

This might mean that while the system requires you to have five priority areas, you choose to bring two of these to the foreground to really push forward effective professional learning and implementation. You can do just enough in the other three areas to satisfy the template's requirements, but internally you should strongly push your top one or two priorities. In our experience, leaders who do this make far more meaningful and measurable progress and are often then held up as exemplars by the system. The key is to hold your nerve in the early stage, and keep your belief that those who pursue less can often achieve far greater impact and sustainable change than those who overload themselves, superficially touching many areas yet achieving no sustainable impact.

9.4 Subtracting to create space for what matters most

For many schools and systems I'm working with, as they progress through three to four successive years of planning and improvement work, they often realise they already have more than enough things to continue with and strengthen in the year ahead, without the need to add anything new. Across those years, leaders and teams also tend to gain much more clarity about what they are "really trying to do". They often come to realise that in the second or third year of a plan, the thing they need most is simply to create space to focus on the small number of things that are most meaningful to the current phase of improvement.

We advise these teams that they might be at a stage where their planning process for the year to come should involve taking the current plan and paring it back to its core essentials. The goal here is to create the bandwidth and focus to secure embedded change in the small number of things they are already convinced are needed next. They don't need to do new data analysis or problem definition. They've already worked out what evidence-informed strategies they can adapt for their unique context. The worst outcome for their change work would be letting this year's plan drag them all the way back into an open stance of searching for new problems to solve. Instead, they should be relentlessly focusing on the things they already know how to do, but haven't yet expanded and embedded into organisational practice.

Our direct guidance to these teams here is clear: add nothing more, and aim to subtract to create space to do what they've already committed to doing – and do it more effectively.

9.5 Listing subtractive improvement strategies in our plan

Believe it or not, in educational settings pruning itself can *be* the short-term improvement strategy all by itself. Subtractive changes can improve the outcomes in and of themselves. Sometimes the best way to add is to delete.

We should be looking for opportunities within our improvement strategies and activities to start listing subtractive changes we will make, for the explicit reason of improving a certain outcome; rather than trying to create space for a new thing. In Chapter 10 we unpack specific guidance on how to run subtractive problem-solving sessions.

9.6 Remember to stay below full capacity as a rule

A common thread of advice throughout the book has been to ensure you don't try to run your team, organisation or system at or above 100% of available capacity in its business-as-usual, steady state. To do so runs the risk that your way of working will become precarious and fragile, resulting in some serious challenges when you need to respond to an unexpected challenge or opportunity. Always leave margin for the unexpected, and with some thinking time baked in to do your job well.

When you set your aspirations for improvement in your plan, ensure that you've calculated that the implementation efforts required will sit under 100% of your team or organisation's capacity. Anything more is imprudent stewardship of your team's resources.

> **Practitioner insights!**
>
> **Making way for priorities**
>
> It is critical that we look at the school as a whole when planning for improvement – and focus on a coherent set of priorities. This can mean cutting back on things that we personally value and are invested in, and working as part of a bigger team. I had invested a lot in developing a school pedagogical model and was ready to roll out whole-staff professional development on it. However, as part of the leadership team, we recognised that having a comprehensive sequenced curriculum that was viable was a higher priority – in fact it was a prerequisite. So that had to be the priority for professional learning. We'll return to the pedagogical model when the time is right.
>
> – Christine Lambrianidis (School leader in Australia)
>
> **Slowing down for the long haul**
>
> A part of pruning improvement for us has been to slow down. I am at the school for the long term and recognise how critical it is to take the time to focus on the most important improvement work and embed it effectively over time. Our initial Annual Improvement Plan (AIP) for this year had too many priorities and strategies. I took six weeks of staff meeting time for all staff to work together on refining our priorities. The end result is a cut-back and focused plan that everyone has engaged deeply with. We've got two clear priorities – and now we're well set up to put them into action.
>
> – Justine Mackey (Principal in Australia)

Deliberately prioritising and pacing change

It is so important to find the right balance in school improvement work. Part of this is getting the pacing right – not taking on too much, and not expecting to go faster than your school can travel. The second part is finding the right balance of things to implement. This can mean putting some work on hold – pruning back on our priorities. We paused implementation of our instructional model to focus on other key improvements that needed to go first. However, we have kept the work progressing with a small, but well-supported, pilot of the instructional model involving a small team of staff. This focused pilot work will then pave the way for when the instructional model does become a whole-school improvement priority in future.

– Veronica Hoy (Principal in Australia)

TIPS FOR PRUNING IMPROVEMENT PLANS

Shift to subtraction first	"It has been a liberating shift to start our annual improvement conversation by looking at what we could stop doing that would address our priorities. We found it helpful not to be looking for silver bullets here – just identify the things, small and large, that would yield improvement from pruning. Not only has it freed up resources, but it has got some key barriers out of the way as well."
Avoid the laundry list	"We've certainly gotten better at this – but there is still a temptation to turn improvement plans into a laundry list of everything you are going to do. Prioritise, prioritise, prioritise. You're still allowed to do things that are not on the list – they are just not your core priority. At the end of the day – if everything is a priority, then nothing is."

Clear the way	"Once we've gone through the comprehensive process of determining our priorities, we need to clear the way for them to be addressed. This has meant postponing, downsizing or removing other initiatives. It can't just be a slash and burn – we've deliberately and repeatedly made the case for cutting back so that we can do our priorities well rather than doing lots of things inadequately."
Just the right data	"We used to include way too much data and too many outcomes. Now we just pick things that we can reliably measure, repeatedly, that directly and clearly link to the priority area and strategy. That way we can tell how we are going, and if we've had an impact – so that our long-term journey is one of informed iterative improvement."
Maintain what matters	"A big part of our pruning of improvement plans has been to shift our thinking about things that are moving into a maintenance phase. We've embedded them and they matter, but now we just need to maintain them. This should take less resources than starting afresh – if it doesn't, something has to change. It seems like a simple thing, but this mindset shift has helped us prune down our initiatives and have a way to talk about keeping the improvement from previous priorities alive and well."

IN SUMMARY

- Don't begin the planning season before engaging in the pruning season.
- The new order of operations for school improvement is subtraction before addition.
- Remember to prune already-embedded activities out into business-as-usual, keeping the plan as simple as possible.

- Sometimes pruning acts as improvement in and of itself, and is all that is needed.
- Remember to stay below 100% capacity as a rule, to allow space to respond to the unexpected.

ON REFLECTION

- Do you make a habit of pruning before planning? If not, how could you create a new rhythm or routine for your team?
- Does the idea of pruning as improvement in itself feel strange to you? What mindset shifts might you need to overcome to embrace this?
- What are some practical ways you can aim to ensure you and your team operate below 100% capacity each year?

CHAPTER 10
SUBTRACTIVE SOLUTION SESSIONS

10.1 Rethinking how to generate solutions

It's time to consider strategic subtraction as a potential improvement strategy for some of the problems we are seeking to solve. We've already seen the benefit of pruning before adding, or subtracting in order to create more space to do the work we are committed to doing – more effectively. In this chapter, we push it further to demonstrate that for many problems we are facing, we could in fact consider pruning *as the improvement strategy*. We explore how to run sessions with your team or full staff to generate solutions, and unpack a simple repeatable process to put more subtractive solutions on the table. Not all problems within education can be solved or outcomes improved through subtractive solutions, but we can make progress on many if we are willing to give subtractive solution sessions a try.

The overlooked power of simple subtractive solutions

As we established in Chapter 1, humans overlook the potential for subtractive solutions when working to solve problems and improve. Author Leidy Klotz makes a convincing argument for this approach in his book *Subtract: The Untapped Science of Less* (Klotz, 2021).

Klotz makes clear that sometimes subtraction can improve outcomes more effectively than addition.

When we learned to ride a bike, our parents took a small, normal-looking bike with pedals and wheels and added training wheels. The logic seemed to be: to improve the experience for kids learning how to ride a bike, we should take the bike and add something. It's a good example of additive thinking: How do we improve this? Training wheels: we add additional wheels to the back of a normal bike.

But these days, you might see toddlers speeding down the street on an odd-looking bike without training wheels or pedals – a balance bike. To make a better bike for a kid to learn on, bike designers realised that the answer was not adding additional wheels at the back but rather subtracting the pedals.

Sometimes, subtraction can make things better. Creating a balance bike – a simpler bike with no pedals – helps young children to learn the most important first step in developing bike riding: to learn how to balance, rather than how to pedal well. It's a great example of how subtraction can make things better, even when it's not the most immediately obvious solution.

Without a subtractive process, we will keep generating additive ideas

When we get our team or broader staff together, our innate tendency to find additive solutions automatically kicks in. People implicitly believe that improvement will require addition beyond everything else we are currently doing, and thus when asked to generate answers will often fill Post-it notes with the next additional thing we should try.

For example, you might raise with your team the challenge of improving teacher wellbeing in your school and ask for suggestions from your leadership team. Ten minutes later, you have collectively generated 10 ideas for additional things that could be put on for teachers in order to lift their wellbeing. You now find yourself committed to running a wellbeing breakfast with yoga starting at 7:15 am on a Wednesday – dragging everybody up and out early – all in the aim of enhancing wellbeing!

How did we find ourselves in such a situation? How might we intentionally interrupt this additive thinking and train ourselves and our teams to think through a subtractive solution lens?

The subtractive solution session process

Running a problem-solving brainstorming session focused exclusively on subtractive solutions is a powerful strategy for fostering innovation and fresh thinking. Unlike traditional brainstorming, which often emphasises additive solutions, this approach challenges participants to identify what can be removed, simplified or eliminated to solve a problem or improve an outcome. This method can help you streamline processes, reduce complexity, and save costs, making it an invaluable tool for teams and schools looking to make progress without adding to their current state of overload.

10.2 There are four steps to subtractive solution sessions

1. Set the scene and prime subtractive thinking

To begin the session, it's crucial to establish the rules of engagement. The facilitator will need to emphasise that all proposed solutions must involve removing, reducing or eliminating elements rather than adding new ones. This can be framed as a creative challenge, encouraging participants to think differently about the problem. Setting this clear boundary helps to focus the group's thinking and encourages a more disciplined approach to problem-solving. It's worth putting up a "No additive solutions" sign that is visible for all.

You could also have a little bell, or even better a squeaky kid's toy, to ring or squeeze when somebody puts forward an additive solution idea. Use the little bell or squeaky toy when somebody suggests an additive solution. If they do it three times in a row, you can have a playful additive timeout chair, where the "offender" needs to sit out of the conversation for one minute before returning. This can be a playful way of helping participants become aware of their additive solution tendencies.

2. Frame the problem to be solved

The facilitator should guide the group through a structured process of getting clear on the focus of the session. Define the problem to be solved or outcome to be improved. Broad starting points might include:

- How could we enhance staff wellbeing through pruning?
- How could we enhance student attendance through pruning?
- How could we support growth and confidence in mathematics through pruning?
- How could we improve our peer review process through pruning?
- How could we improve the efficiency of our collaborative planning through pruning?

Start by encouraging participants to identify the core elements of the problem and then try to be as specific as possible. Be open to the potential of reframing the problem together, or focusing on a smaller slice of the broader challenge – for example, moving from "How can we improve attendance?" to "How can we lift on-time school arrival for Year 9 and 10 boys with a track record of less than 30% attendance over the past year?" Once the problem is clearly framed and understood, write it as a clear problem statement on the board.

Table 10.1: Terms to stimulate subtractive ideas

Pruning	Scaling down	Condensing
Decreasing	Omitting	Easing off
Subtracting	Shrinking	Reducing
Taking away	Simplifying	Removing
Minimising	Diminishing	Eliminating
Cutting	Streamlining	Downsizing
Trimming	Shortening	Erasing

3. Generate ideas individually and then collectively

During the brainstorming session, give members of the group time to generate as many subtractive ideas as possible on their own Post-it notes, or alternatively on your choice of digital platform, to capture initial ideas. During this phase, the goal is to generate as many subtractive ideas as possible without judging or evaluating their likely impact or effort.

You might find it useful to have a set of subtractive prompts stuck up on a wall to help people prime the right type of thinking – for example, "We could make progress on this problem by…" (see Table 10.1).

The facilitator can also use some additional question prompts to help stimulate fresh subtractive thinking:

- Which aspects of our current approach might be unnecessary or overly complicated?
- What could be taken away to achieve the desired outcome?
- Which steps in our process could be simplified or eliminated without compromising significant impact?
- What elements of our approach are adding complexity without delivering significant marginal value?
- How can we streamline our approach to focus only on what truly matters and still get most of the upside?
- Are there any resources or tools we're using that might be redundant or unneeded?
- What steps, tasks or components could we remove to make our approach more efficient?

The lateral thinking approach here might seem strange initially, but as you begin to work with your team, you might find answers in unexpected places. The facilitator should also periodically remind the team of the subtractive focus, helping to steer the conversation away from additive suggestions. Ring the bell or squeeze the squeaky toy as needed, to help people become aware of any drift into their default additive ideas.

After the individual idea generation, individuals can share their Post-it notes, work together to delete or combine identical ideas, and then cluster together similar ideas into groups.

4. Discuss, categorise and unpack subtractive change ideas

The group can now review, discuss and categorise the proposed subtractive solutions, evaluating their potential positive impact and the effort that might be required to carry out the subtractive change. Prioritise the ideas that offer the most significant potential benefits with the least risk or unnecessary change burden. Map these out clearly as a set of potential pruning targets that can be carried out.

Consider and map out the underlying pathway by which the suggested subtractive change could have a positive impact on the identified problem. You should also identify the likely "lead indicators" that should improve first if the change is going well. In project management, lead indicators are established to help us gauge progress; they're the first key things that should start moving, improving or changing, and they should be measurable and achievable.

Concluding the session with a clear summary of the brainstorming outputs and some tangible suggestions will reinforce the value of everyone's contribution and set everyone up for an effective course of action through the Remove and Nurture phases of the pruning cycle.

10.3 Activate steps in "consciously remove" and "carefully nurture"

Once you've moved through the subtractive problem-solving session and generated some ideas, you can then move on to the Remove and Nurture steps of the pruning cycle. As we all know with pruning, generating fresh subtractive ideas is insufficient. It's essential to carefully plan out the removal and nurturing process to avoid unintended consequences.

As you run more "subtractive answers only" problem-solving sessions, you'll soon find that people will be able to generate some really interesting and different approaches. It might be just the approach needed to unlock fresh thinking, energy and momentum in your team.

TIPS FOR SUBTRACTIVE PROBLEM-SOLVING

Flip the script	Challenge the team to reverse their usual approach. Instead of adding more, ask them to think about what could be taken away. This inversion sparks creativity and pushes the team to explore ideas they might not consider in a traditional session. In a subtractive session, even small ideas can have a big impact. Encourage the team to value and share any reduction, no matter how minor.
Maintain tight constraints	Set clear guidelines that only subtractive ideas are allowed. These constraints aren't limitations – they're creative fuel. When everyone is focused on reduction, the group is more likely to find innovative, streamlined solutions.
Embrace simplicity	Guide your team to think in terms of simplicity. Encourage them to ask, "What can we remove to make this better?" It's about focusing on the essence of the problem and stripping away the excess to reveal the core solution.
Visualise the before and after	Help the team see the difference subtraction makes by visualising what it will look like after pruning. Whether it's a process flowchart, a storyboard, or just a list, showing the "before" and "after" highlights the effectiveness of subtractive thinking and keeps the team focused on making tangible shifts that impact the lives of the people involved.

IN SUMMARY

- Subtractive solutions can be more effective than additive ones. A perfect example is the invention of the balance bike instead of adding training wheels.

- Subtractive problem-solving sessions provide a structured way for your team to learn to think in subtractive ways.

- Start by setting the scene for how to engage in the session ("subtractive ideas only"), then frame the problem to be solved (make it specific), and aim to generate ideas individually and collectively.

- Discuss, categorise and unpack your ideas, then shortlist them as pruning targets.

- Phases 2 and 3 of the cycle – Consciously Remove and Carefully Nurture – then apply as usual. See Chapter 3 for guidances on these these steps.

ON REFLECTION

- When would be an ideal time for you to run your first subtractive solution session?

- What might your team find hardest about a session like this, and how could you mitigate it?

CONCLUSION

As educators and school leaders, it is time to start engaging together in pruning. It needs to become habitual and baked in as an automatic part of our yearly cycles, because while mastering the art of strategic subtraction may seem simple in theory, the collective impact it can have on our roles, teams and schools is nearly limitless. We would go so far as to say that we believe we will reach our next improvement stage as educators only once we discover how to prune. Our schools are organisations that are built for the long term. This means we need them to thrive not just over the next few years, but over the coming decades. If our schools are going to have a sustainable impact for multiple decades and be set up for real success, it's imperative that we learn how to *intentionally stop doing things*. Even when it's uncomfortable. Even when it hurts. And even when we've sunk a lot of energy and investment into something. We must learn to reach for the secateurs and build the muscle memory for cutting back, not because our various activities aren't worthy, but because we've learned to what extent good can be the enemy of great.

As we've explored, schools are playing a zero-sum game with financial and human resources. It's simply not sustainable to continue to deplete both of those and continue to burn through the goodwill and energy of our staff. It's dicey, and we know it. We feel that tension of being stretched too thin each term keenly, and we can observe its impact among our colleagues. Pursuing an unrealistic number of things to do is the swiftest pathway to less-effective schools and less-motivated staff. We need to discipline ourselves to start applying the Pruning Principle – regularly. We need to discover the mindset, process and tools behind pruning, and hold ourselves accountable to the process of auditing our activities and committing to doing fewer things. Like any new habit, it will feel awkward at first, it will take time to cement, and there will be trial and error along the way. But the payoff is too great for our schools to ignore.

This is a novel way of thinking for many of us who have a strong moral imperative and a desire to make an impact. As we have unpacked in this book, we tend to implicitly believe that seeking to improve something equates to adding to it while continuing on with everything we are already doing as well. However, the Pruning Principle suggests that while such thinking seems correct at face value in our quest for impact, when we look more closely, it in fact hampers a school's long-term growth, vitality and structural integrity. We have uncovered a counter-cultural reality that more is *not* always more. And in fact, the best way to achieve more in our overloaded schools might actually be to systematically do less.

The inverse is also true. When we avoid pruning our activities, or worse, engage in continual additive growth, we actually reduce our educational institution's long-term growth. By pruning regularly, we are deciding to unlock our school's potential for fresh growth and vitality.

How pruning serves the vision

As leaders, our job is to set vision. We define the reality of the day-to-day culture and work life for many of our colleagues, we establish shared goals, and we set the intention for the kind of school or system we want to be. The beautiful insight from the Pruning Principle when we apply it to our living systems is that through the pursuit of less, we actually achieve far more. It's the most effective method of having greater sustainable impact long term. If we could do fewer things better, we would both enhance the impact that we have on children and young people, and manage to sustain the types of cultures that are worth working in for a long time for the adults who serve in education. The staff retention upside to pruning is immense. Imagine a culture where staff were motivated, energised and had spare bandwidth to pursue opportunities as they arose. This is the impact of pruning.

It's time to ask ourselves new questions about how we can make things better through strategic subtraction. How could we renew, energise and improve the bandwidth of our people by pruning back our activities and commitments? How might we build vision, alignment and a sense of coherence within our schools that is even more compelling through pruning? Pruning is the missing piece for becoming laser-focused on the things that best serve the vision we have for our schools.

As you've read this book, you've no doubt already been thinking about what pruning might look like in your patch of the educational landscape. We'd love to hear from you and connect you with other practitioners from around the world. Please visit https://pruningprinciple.com to connect, gain inspiration, and share your insights on mastering strategic subtraction in education.

Case study: Beginning pruning at Cranbourne East Primary School

Cranbourne East Primary School is a large government school in suburban Melbourne, Victoria, Australia. School leaders Chanel Herring, Sarah Kubik and David Muzyk worked through a comprehensive process to begin educational pruning at their school. After learning about the core concepts, they moved readily into action in order to build their pruning capabilities and culture through a series of collective pruning experiments.

Initiating the Pruning Cycle

The team took time and care to get the framing right and get everyone on the same page as to the what and why of educational pruning. This set the scene for open and transparent discussions and helped everyone to connect pruning to the broader journey of school improvement. This included:

- **Previewing pruning** – letting everyone know a few weeks ahead of time to allow everyone time to reflect in advance.

- **Unpacking the concept** – explaining the pruning concept, its connections to school improvement, and everyone's role in contributing.
- **Framing the opportunity** – making it clear that this was an opportunity for everyone's voice to be heard and that nothing was too precious or off the table.
- **Setting the tone** – emphasising that honesty was welcomed and that it was a non-judgemental process.

Critically examining

For their first go at whole-school pruning, the team made some deliberate decisions to set up a workable process to identify and categorise targets. This included:

- **Working in small teams to examine** – facilitating sessions in small teams that worked closely together to identify and categorise pruning targets. This provided workable group sizes for meaningful discussion and capitalised on the shared expertise and existing trust within each team.
- **Looking at three specific areas** – focusing on administration, teaching and learning and wellbeing. Running a separate session on each helped to focus the pruning process. Keeping the process consistent each time helped people to get into the rhythm.
- **Providing possible targets** – providing a starting point by identifying likely targets in each area based on existing feedback data. This helped to kick-start the additional targets and provide a starting point for discussion that followed.
- **Categorising targets** – using three simple and consistent categories: cut, trim or cherish. Staff were provided with cards to represent each area. For each target they held up the card to show their recommended course of action.

This was a simple and clear structure to introduce pruning as well as a fun way for everyone to engage.
- **Discussion as part of forming consensus** – unpacking the reasoning behind cutting, pruning or nurturing. Recording the different perspectives raised in discussion helped to inform pruning decisions.

Having captured comprehensive input from all staff in the school, the team then set about prioritising pruning targets. As this was the first pruning cycle, there was an immense amount of input – they used a digital tool to create a detailed dashboard to bring it all together and prioritise. This included:

- **Drawing on other data** – combining staff input from the pruning process with other feedback from existing staff opinion surveys and other available data. This built a bigger picture of the targets to help with decision-making.
- **Starting with the burning issues** – prioritising those targets that were clearly high priority first and then working through the complete list from there.
- **Considering timing** – looking at factors that would impact when something could be changed. For example, changes to reporting and parent–teacher interviews could not be actioned until the following year because of what was already in place.

Next steps

The next steps that the team took looked towards the Remove and Nurture phases, while also making the most of opportunities to establish an ongoing pruning culture within the school. This included:

- **Empowering teams to prune at their level** – where a target related to a specific team, not the whole school, giving that team explicit permission to action it themselves immediately.

- **Making a pruning action plan** – getting clear on what action would be taken, who was responsible, and when it would be done.
- **Communicating back to staff** – providing visibility of the outputs of the critical examination process, plus the actions taken, and timeframes.
- **Monitoring pruning progress** – tracking progress against the pruning action plan and gaining feedback on the impact of initial pruning efforts.
- **Setting the scene for a regular cadence** – looking ahead to revisiting whole-school pruning as a part of the annual improvement cycle – communicating with staff that this was not a one-off and would be a regular process in future.
- **Considering more detailed examination** – exploring ways to go deeper in further cycles to evaluate workload, impact and other factors to help identify pruning targets – particularly within teaching and learning and wellbeing.

This is just the start of the pruning journey at Cranbourne East Primary School – the thoughtful approach that the team has put in place has set them up well, and we look forward to hearing more of their journey in future.

APPENDICES

Appendix A: Existing work on de-implementation

The Pruning Principle is connected to, yet stands apart from, the concept of de-implementation. Existing research and practice in de-implementation relate to the broader field of implementation and are more commonly focused on healthcare and human services. De-implementation has also become a topic for exploration recently in education. Some key works in both education and healthcare that explore aspects of de-implementation are briefly summarised below:

Healthcare and implementation science

- *Evidence-based de-implementation for contradicted, unproven, and aspiring healthcare practices* (Prasad & Ioannidis, 2014) – an examination of the concept of evidence-based de-implementation in healthcare including defining de-implementation as abandoning ineffective practices, three categories (contradicted, unproven, novel), challenges, areas for further effort, and some healthcare-specific examples.
- *Working smarter not harder: Coupling implementation to de-implementation* (Wang et al., 2018) – an exploration of connections between implementation and de-implementation, including types of de-implementation (partial reduction, complete

reversal, substitution) and the role of learning and unlearning in the process of change.

- *Letting go: Conceptualising intervention de-implementation in public health and social service settings* (McKay et al., 2018) – an examination of the concept of de-implementation in public health and social services which proposes a definition, unpacks criteria for selecting interventions to de-implement (ineffective, harmful, low value, no longer needed), explores frameworks for putting this into action, and highlights the importance of a process-based approach, consideration of contextual factors, and sustainability.
- *Defining and conceptualising outcomes for de-implementation: Key distinctions from implementation outcomes* (Prusaczyk et al., 2020) – an exploration of de-implementation outcomes (acceptability, adoption, appropriateness, cost, feasibility, fidelity, penetration, and sustainability).
- *A scoping review of de-implementation frameworks and models* (Walsh-Bailey et al., 2021) – an examination of frameworks and models for de-implementation across various disciplines.
- *Determinants of the de-implementation of low-value care: A multi-method study* (Parsons Leigh et al., 2022) – a study of determinants impacting de-implementation efforts, specifically looking at barriers (lack of credible evidence, entrenched norms, resistance to change) and facilitators (stakeholder collaboration, communication and availability of credible evidence).

Education

- *Northern Territory de-implementation guide* (Evidence for Learning, 2020) – a guide developed for the Northern Territory Department of Education focused on system-level change that explores four types of de-implementation (reverse, reduce, replace, rethink) for practices that are not evidence-based and enacting this through adapting an existing four-stage approach to implementation (explore, prepare, deliver, sustain).
- *Insights into de-implementation* (Evidence for Learning, 2022) – an exploration of the application of de-implementation to education

including potential benefits, a four-stage process (explore, prepare, deliver, sustain), drawing on evidence to inform decisions, and considerations for doing so effectively.
- *Doing fewer things, better: The case for de-implementation* (Schoeffel & Rosenbrock, 2022) – a summary of what de-implementation is in the education context, what evidence can be drawn on in undertaking it, a four-stage process for putting it into practice, and key considerations for school leaders.
- *De-implementation: Creating the space to focus on what works* (DeWitt, 2022) – an education-focused exploration of types of de-implementation and an associated cycle.
- *Making room for impact: A guide to de-implementation for educators* (Hamilton et al., 2023) – a framework for de-implementation applied to education across a four-step process (discover, decide, de-implement, re-decide).

Appendix B: Drawing on evidence when making decisions

Evidence can help us to uncover potential for impact based on what has worked and is "critical in the exercise of professional judgement" (Deeble & Vaughan, 2022). This may be focused on student academic and wellbeing outcomes, or another measure specifically aligned to an objective. Evidence-informed decisions integrate "professional expertise with the best external evidence from research to improve the quality of practice" (Sharples, 2013).

There are two broad categories of evidence we may draw on to inform practice.

1. *Practice-based evidence* identifies the current impact of a practice as implemented in your school, and the details that contribute to this. This is collected by educators in your setting – it is specific to your context and can tell you what is actually happening in practice. As it is also something you can gather yourself, it can be

very useful for digging deeper into a particular focus area to help inform decision-making.

2. *Research evidence* identifies the potential impact (positive or negative) of a particular approach, the core features that contribute to the effect, and the circumstances in which it has been shown to be effective (Evidence for Learning, 2024). Not all research evidence can provide equal levels of confidence of impact. We can place higher levels of confidence on systematic reviews that draw together many studies, as well as experimental studies such as randomised control trials (Deeble & Vaughan, 2022). Other evidence may point us to what could work, but with less confidence, or unpack the details of how something may be effective in practice. With any evidence it is important to approach it with a critical perspective – being aware of any potential for bias and being wary of claims.

When looking to dive deeper into research evidence, the following organisations can provide a good starting point:

- What Works Clearinghouse (USA)
  https://ies.ed.gov/ncee/wwc
- Education Endowment Foundation (UK)
  https://educationendowmentfoundation.org.uk
- Evidence for Learning (Australia)
  https://evidenceforlearning.org.au
- Australian Education Research Organisation
  https://www.edresearch.edu.au
- Evidence for Education Network (International)
  https://evidence.education

Appendix C: The Pruning Matrix

Area of focus | Date

	WEAKER IMPACT	STRONGER IMPACT
LOWER EFFORT		
HIGHER EFFORT		

Appendix D: The Pruning Cycle Planning Tool

In each box map out the: 1. People you will work with, 2. Tools you will use and, 3. Actions you will take

Area of focus	Date	Team

1. Critically Examine	2. Consciously Remove	3. Carefully Nurture
A. Identify pruning targets	A. Attune to people and environment	A. Protect the space
B. Categorise and evaluate	B. Communicate the narrative	B. Fertilise and champion
C. Prioritise and sequence	C. Steward the change	C. Seek feedback and monitor impact

REFERENCES

Adams, G. S., Converse, B. A., Hales, A. H., & Klotz, L. E. (2021). People systematically overlook subtractive changes. *Nature, 592*(7853), 258–61. https://doi.org/10.1038/s41586-021-03380-y

Arkes, H. R., & Blumer, C. (1985). The psychology of sunk cost. *Organizational Behavior and Human Decision Processes, 35*(1), 124–40. https://doi.org/10.1016/0749-5978(85)90049-4

Australian Institute for Teaching and School Leadership. (2024). *National Trends Teacher Workforce*. AITSL. https://www.aitsl.edu.au/research/australian-teacher-workforce-data/atwd-reports/national-trends-teacher-workforce

Botsman, R. (2023, March 20). How to *not* be a people pleaser [Substack newsletter]. *Rethink with Rachel.* https://rachelbotsman.substack.com/p/how-to-not-be-a-people-pleaser

Cole, P. (2012). *Linking Effective Professional Learning with Effective Teaching Practice.* Australian Institute for Teaching and School Leadership.

Cordingley, P., Higgins, S., Greaney, T., Buckler, N., Coles-Jordan, D., Crisp, B., Saunders, L., & Coe, R. (2015). *Developing Great Teaching: Lessons from the International Reviews into Effective Professional Development.* Teacher Development Trust. https://tdtrust.org/about/dgt/

Curtis, P. (2003, June 20). Teachers put off by initiative overload. *The Guardian.* https://www.theguardian.com/education/2003/jun/20/schools.uk3

Deeble, M., & Vaughan, T. (2018). *An Evidence Broker for Australian Schools.* CSE, Occasional Paper 155. https://evidenceforlearning.org.au/about-us/position-papers-and-articles/an-evidence-broker-for-australian-schools

Dewitt, P. (2022). *De-implementation: Creating the Space to Focus on What Works.* Corwin.

Education Endowment Foundation. (2021). *Effective Professional Development.* Education Endowment Foundation (EEF). https://educationendowmentfoundation.org.uk/education-evidence/guidance-reports/effective-professional-development

Education Endowment Foundation. (2023). *Review of Evidence on Teacher Quality, Recruitment and Retention*. Education Endowment Foundation (EEF). https://educationendowmentfoundation.org.uk/education-evidence/evidence-reviews/teacher-quality-recruitment-and-retention

Evidence for Learning. (2020). *Northern Territory De-implementation Guide*. https://evidenceforlearning.org.au/support-for-implementation/nt-school-improvement-hub/northern-territory-guidance-reports#nav-a-guide-to-de-implementation

Evidence for Learning. (2022). *Insights into De-implementation*. Evidence for Learning.

Evidence for Learning. (2024). *Planning for Impact 2024*. Evidence for Learning. https://evidenceforlearning.org.au/support-for-implementation/school-planning-and-recovery/planning-for-impact-2024

Galai, D., & Sade, O. (2005). *The "Ostrich Effect" and the Relationship between the Liquidity and the Yields of Financial Assets* (SSRN Scholarly Paper No. 666163). https://doi.org/10.2139/ssrn.666163

Hamilton, A., Hattie, J., & William, D. (2023). *Making Room for Impact: A Guide to De-implementation for Educators*. Corwin.

Heffernan, A., Bright, D., Longmuir, F., & Kim, M. (2019). *Perceptions of Teachers and Teaching in Australia*. Monash University. https://www.monash.edu/education/teachspace/articles/how-do-australias-teachers-feel-about-their-work

Horowitz, L. L., Parker, K., & Menasce, J. (2024, April 4). How teachers manage their workload. *Pew Research Center*. https://www.pewresearch.org/social-trends/2024/04/04/how-teachers-manage-their-workload/

Hsu, A. (2023, February 15). Shopify deleted 322,000 hours of meetings. Should the rest of us be jealous? *NPR*. https://www.npr.org/2023/02/15/1156804295/shopify-delete-meetings-zoom-virtual-productivity

Hunter, J., Sonnemann, J., & Joiner, R. (2021). *Results of the 2021 Grattan Survey on Teachers' Time*. Grattan Institute.

Kahneman, D. (2013). *Thinking, Fast and Slow* (1st Ed.). Farrar, Straus and Giroux.

Klotz, L. (2021). *Subtract: The Untapped Science of Less*. St Martin's Press. https://www.amazon.com.au/Subtract-Untapped-Science-Leidy-Klotz/dp/1250249864

McGregor, J. (2023, January 23). *This Company Is Canceling All Meetings with More Than Two Employees to Free Up Workers' Time*. Forbes. https://www.forbes.com/sites/jenamcgregor/2023/01/03/shopify-is-canceling-all-meetings-with-more-than-two-people-from-workers-calendars-and-urging-few-to-be-added-back/

McKay, V. R., Morshed, A. B., Brownson, R. C., Proctor, E. K., & Prusaczyk, B. (2018). Letting go: Conceptualising intervention de-implementation in public health and social service settings. *American Journal of Community Psychology*, *62*(1–2), 189–202. https://doi.org/10.1002/ajcp.12258

McKeown, G. (2014). *Essentialism: The Disciplined Pursuit of Less*. Crown Business.

National Geographic Society. (2024). *Traces of Ancient Rome in the Modern World*. https://education.nationalgeographic.org/resource/traces-ancient-rome-modern-world

NSW Department of Education. (2017). *Principal Workload and Time Use Study*. NSW Department of Education. https://education.nsw.gov.au/content/dam/main-education/en/home/gef1/media/documents/Principal-workload-and-time-use-study-Nov-2017.pdf

OECD. (2021). *Teachers Getting the Best out of Their Students: From Primary to Upper Secondary Education*. OECD. https://doi.org/10.1787/5bc5cd4e-en

Parsons Leigh, J., Sypes, E., Straus, S., Demiantschuk, D., Ma, H., Brundin-Mather, R., Grood, C., FitzGerald, E., Mizen, S., Stelfox, H., & Niven, D. (2022). Determinants of the de-implementation of low-value care: A multi-method study. *BMC Health Services Research*, *22*. https://doi.org/10.1186/s12913-022-07827-4

Pliny, the Elder. (n.d.). *The Natural History of Pliny, Volume 4 (of 6) by Pliny, the Elder*. Project Gutenberg. https://www.gutenberg.org/files/61113/61113-h/61113-h.htm

Porter, M. E. (1996). What Is Strategy? *Harvard Business Review*, November–December 1996. https://hbr.org/1996/11/what-is-strategy

Prasad, V., & Ioannidis, J. P. (2014). Evidence-based de-implementation for contradicted, unproven, and aspiring healthcare practices. *Implementation Science*, *9*(1), 1. https://doi.org/10.1186/1748-5908-9-1

Prusaczyk, B., Swindle, T., & Curran, G. (2020). Defining and conceptualising outcomes for de-implementation: Key distinctions from implementation outcomes. *Implementation Science Communications*, *1*(1), 43. https://doi.org/10.1186/s43058-020-00035-3

Samuelson, W., & Zeckhauser, R. (1988). Status quo bias in decision making. *Journal of Risk and Uncertainty*, *1*(1), 7–59. https://doi.org/10.1007/BF00055564

Schoeffel, S., & Rosenbrock, M. (2022). Doing fewer things, better: The case for de-implementation. *Teacher Magazine*. https://www.teachermagazine.com/au_en/articles/doing-fewer-things-better-the-case-for-de-implementation

Sharot, T. (2011). The optimism bias. *Current Biology*, *21*(23), R941–R945. https://doi.org/10.1016/j.cub.2011.10.030

Sharples, D. J. (2013). *Evidence for the Frontline: A Report for the Alliance for Useful Evidence*. Alliance for Useful Evidence.

Timperley, H., Wilson, A., Barrar, H., & Fung, I. (2007). *Teacher Professional Learning and Development: Best Evidence Synthesis Iteration (BES)*. New

Zealand Ministry of Education. https://www.educationcounts.govt.nz/publications/series/2515/15341

Walsh-Bailey, C., Tsai, E., Tabak, R. G., Morshed, A. B., Norton, W. E., McKay, V. R., Brownson, R. C., & Gifford, S. (2021). A scoping review of de-implementation frameworks and models. *Implementation Science*, *16*(1), 100. https://doi.org/10.1186/s13012-021-01173-5

Wang, V., Maciejewski, M. L., Helfrich, C. D., & Weiner, B. J. (2018). Working smarter not harder: Coupling implementation to de-implementation. *Healthcare*, *6*(2), 104–107. https://doi.org/10.1016/j.hjdsi.2017.12.004

Wason, P. (1960). On the Failure to Eliminate Hypotheses in a Conceptual Task. *Quarterly Journal of Experimental Psychology*, 12(3), 129–40. https://journals.sagepub.com/doi/10.1080/17470216008416717

Weinstein, N. D. (1980). Unrealistic optimism about future life events. *Journal of Personality and Social Psychology*, *39*(5), 806–20. https://doi.org/10.1037/0022-3514.39.5.806

William, D. (2018, November 13). [Tweet]. Twitter. https://x.com/dylanwiliam/status/1062144139993776128

INDEX

3D Reset Tool 76, 84

action research projects 102, 109–110
adding 8, 10–16, 19, 51, 86, 128
addition 8, 10–12, 15, 118–119, 128–129
additive trap 2, 7–16
administration 63–64, 93–94, 96, 138
alignment 85, 89, 111, 137
ancient Greeks 17–18
ancient Romans 17–18
attune 44–45
avoid pruning 27–28, 54, 136

bandwidth 77–78, 119, 137
benefits 32, 38–41, 43, 52, 57, 132
blackout periods 90, 100
boundaries 15, 78, 83
budget 103–104
building 37, 59–60, 77–78
busy 7–8, 15

cadence 87, 90, 94, 140
calendar 8, 74, 77–78, 82, 85, 88, 91, 96–97, 99
calm 1, 3
capability 77–78
capacity 8, 47–48, 72, 78, 111–114, 118, 122–123, 126

care 10, 14, 31–32, 44, 52
carefully nurture 31–34, 47–49, 94–97, 132, 146
caring more 52, 58
case study 137–140
categorise 34, 36, 38–42, 110–112, 131, 138, 146
champion 33–34, 48, 95–96, 108, 146
change 13, 24, 32, 34, 42–46, 49, 51–52, 61–62, 77, 83, 121–122, 124, 131–132, 146
change fatigue 13, 44
classroom observation 105
cognitive bias 53, 55–56
collaboration 93
collapse 87, 90
communicate 34, 45–46, 146
confirmation bias 55
connection 13, 111
consciously remove 31–34, 44–46, 77, 91, 132, 146
cooling off 88
coordination levy 12, 16
Cranbourne East Primary School 137–140
critically examine 31–44, 74, 89–91, 109–110, 146
cultivate 31, 47–48
curiosity 60, 79

151

cutting back 18–19, 21, 91–95, 104, 123
cutting off 18, 20, 91–92, 104

data 49, 63, 65, 125, 139
de-implementation 2, 141–143
delay 76
delegation 76–78
delete 89
difficulties 39–40
discipline 78–79
doing less 2, 18, 48, 52
doing more 1, 7–8, 10, 52, 58
dump 76, 80
duplication 96

Education Endowment Foundation 111, 114
educator workload 9
effectiveness 101–102, 105, 111
effort 14, 32, 38, 41–42, 48, 56–57, 106, 110, 115, 120, 145
email 81–83, 93–94, 98
email surcharge 12, 16
embeddedness 42, 44
examine 31–44, 79, 88–89, 102–103, 109–110, 120, 146
experiments 59–67, 73–74, 79

fear of missing out (FOMO) 72
feedback 34, 49, 64–65, 94, 110–111, 146
fertilise 33–34, 48, 146
financial 41
finite energy 20–21
focus 3, 24, 34, 36, 54, 71, 93–95, 113–114, 123–124, 133
framing 130, 138
frenzied stagnation 7–8, 15, 72
frequent initiatives 13
full capacity 12, 72, 122–123

gains 86–87
generating ideas 37, 130–131

good enough 43, 112

health 19–20, 23–24
healthcare 141–142
hidden costs 12, 16
horticulture 17, 19–21, 25
human effort 41

identify 36–38, 109, 138, 146
impact 18, 48–49, 51, 54–57, 89, 94, 110, 135–137, 145–146
implementation science 141–142
improvement 2, 10, 16, 63, 101, 117–127
improvement plans 117–126
influence 35, 42, 55
initiating 34–35, 137–128
initiative overload 13
instructional coaching 110
intentional subtraction 19, 88
interruptions 66
investment 52–53

judgement 40, 43, 143

Klotz, Leidy 127–128

language 45–46, 61
leadership 63–64, 89, 96–97
light targeted pruning 27
lists 15, 47, 82
longevity 20, 23–24
long-term vitality 18–19, 80

maintenance effort 14
major pruning 26
making decisions 9, 38, 143–144
manageability 60–61
McKeown, Greg 72
meeting schedule 97–98
meeting-reduction 89–93
meeting-reduction map 91
meetings 63, 85–100
mindset shifts 2, 51–57

152 THE PRUNING PRINCIPLE

mindsets 79
monitoring 49, 146
more 8–14

new growth 19–22
next 43, 76–77, 112–113, 139
no 57–58, 78, 82, 117
normal 7, 128
now 43, 76–77, 119
nurture 31–34, 47–49, 73, 79, 88, 94–95, 132, 139, 146

olive trees 17
on hold 43
operations 63–64
optimism bias 55
options 32, 34–36, 38–39, 77, 79, 81, 110–112
organisations 23–26, 32, 119, 122
ostrich effect 56
outcomes 41, 142
overload 7, 13, 72, 76, 117–118
overloaded plans 117–118

pacing 46, 124
pandemic 12, 14
PD share-backs 113
PD-pruning cycle 109–110
people management tax 16
permission 48, 79–81, 83
personal pruning 24–25, 71–84
personal workload 3, 24, 63
plans 117–125
PLCs 38, 106–107, 113
Pliny the Elder 18
Porter, Michael 117
post-pandemic 12, 14
previous mistakes 52–53
priorities 24–25, 39, 43, 97, 111–112, 119, 123–125
prioritising 43, 75, 77, 82, 112, 124, 139
professional development 63, 101–116

progress 7, 49, 88, 120–121, 140
protect 34, 47–48, 52, 78–79, 99, 146
pruning
    experiments 2, 59–67, 73–74, 77
    meetings 3, 85–100
    rhythms 24–26
    targets 32, 34–40, 75–76, 89, 104, 146
Pruning Cycle, The 2–3, 31–50, 62, 74–78, 102, 146
Pruning Cycle Planning Tool, The 62, 146
Pruning in Action 2, 69
Pruning Matrix, The 110, 145
purpose 23, 89, 98, 114

redirects 20–21, 28
reduce 41, 61, 76, 88, 90–92
refine 90
refocusing 94
regular rhythms 19, 73–74
removing 20, 31–34, 44–46, 96, 112
reporting 64–65
reshapes 20, 23–24, 28
resistance to change 13, 142
review 31, 35–38, 74, 89
rhythm 1, 24–26, 73–74, 118–119
right people 95

safe entry points 61
school environment 46, 64
seasonal thinking 26–27
sequencing 77
Shopify 88
significance 42
simplicity 3, 49, 133
size 38
slowing down 123
social contract 15
solution sessions 127–134
space 34, 47–48, 78–79, 90, 96, 121–122, 146
stagnation 7–8, 72
start small 60, 74, 112–113

status-quo bias 55
stewarding change 46
stimulates 20–22, 28
student
    engagement 64
    wellbeing 64
subtracting 44, 121–122
subtractive
    change 16, 62, 122, 131–132
    solutions 3, 127–134
    thinking 129–131
success 59–61
sunk cost 53–55, 58, 115
sunk cost fallacy 55
sustainability 2, 142
system-level pruning 24–25

taking away 52, 130
teaching and learning 64
team-level pruning 24–25
technology 64, 66
temptation 52–53
the additive trap 2, 7–16

The Pruning Cycle 2–3, 31–50, 62, 74–78, 102, 146
The Pruning Cycle Planning Tool 62, 146
The Pruning Matrix 110, 145
The Pruning Principle 2, 5–67
thinking 26–27, 39, 43, 51, 56–57, 110, 115, 129, 131–132
time 41, 43, 72–82, 86–88, 90–99, 101–115
timing 18, 25, 28, 43, 96, 111–112, 139
trade-offs 9, 56, 94

vision 23, 55, 136–137
visualise 133

Wiliam, Dylan 57
workflow 25, 63, 71–81
workload 9, 24, 63, 71–81

yes 56–57, 74, 107